The Making of the Modern Chinese Navy

The Making of the Modern Chinese Navy

Special Historical Characteristics

Bruce A. Elleman

ANTHEM PRESS

Anthem Press
An imprint of Wimbledon Publishing Company
www.anthempress.com

This edition first published in UK and USA 2019
by ANTHEM PRESS
75–76 Blackfriars Road, London SE1 8HA, UK
or PO Box 9779, London SW19 7ZG, UK
and
244 Madison Ave #116, New York, NY 10016, USA

Copyright © Bruce A. Elleman 2019

The author asserts the moral right to be identified as the author of this work.

All rights reserved. Without limiting the rights under copyright reserved above, no part of this publication may be reproduced, stored or introduced into a retrieval system, or transmitted, in any form or by any means (electronic, mechanical, photocopying, recording or otherwise), without the prior written permission of both the copyright owner and the above publisher of this book.

British Library Cataloguing-in-Publication Data
A catalogue record for this book is available from the British Library.

ISBN-13: 978-1-78527-100-7 (Hbk)
ISBN-10: 1-78527-100-8 (Hbk)

This title is also available as an e-book.

CONTENTS

	Introduction: The Special Characteristics of China's Maritime History	1
1.	Battle of Bạch Đằng River (938)	7
2.	Battle of Yaishan (1279)	11
3.	Battle of Lake Poyang (1363)	17
4.	Ming–Kotte War in Southeast Asia (1410–11)	21
5.	Ming Loyalists Flee to Taiwan (1661–83)	25
6.	Battle of Chuanbi (1839)	29
7.	Sino-French War (1884–85)	35
8.	Qing Beiyang Fleet's Defeat in the Battle of the Yellow Sea (1894)	39
9.	Chinese Decision to Sink The Nationalist Navy as Blockships (1937)	43
10.	*Chongqing* Mutiny Allowing the PLA to Cross the Yangzi River (1949)	47
11.	The Taiwan Strait Crises (1954–55 and 1958)	51
12.	China's Decision to Take the Paracel Islands from South Vietnam (1974)	57
13.	Missile Blockade: The Taiwan Strait Crisis (1995–96)	63
14.	The EP-3 Standoff and Diplomatic Resolution (2001)	69
	Conclusions: The Influence of History on the Formation of a Modern Chinese Navy	73
Selected Bibliography		83
Index		87

INTRODUCTION: THE SPECIAL CHARACTERISTICS OF CHINA'S MARITIME HISTORY

Like all countries with a long maritime tradition, there are many unique ways each country's navy fight. The US Navy, for example, is known for never giving up. It still honors John Paul Jones's famous saying "I have not yet begun to fight." In 1905, Jones's body was even exhumed from a Parisian cemetery and reburied in the Annapolis chapel to symbolize the importance of this American characteristic. Other global navies have their own ingrained beliefs, some of which defy reason, including the Royal Navy half-gill ration of grog per day or how Japanese pilots preferred death, many opting not to bring a parachute with them on missions, to the dishonor of military defeat. The focus of this book will be on those special characteristics that distinguish the Chinese navy.

The fourteen historical case studies presented below will help to illustrate a number of special characteristics that modern-day Chinese naval officers perhaps take for granted, including a belief in the Mandate of Heaven, tributary system, and the fear of "losing face," either in a diplomatic setting, in a military defeat, or by risking valuable equipment in battle. Ethnic and language differences, regional loyalties, and political mistrust potentially exacerbate these problems. Peculiarities include the Mongol dual-officer diarchy that led to political commissar system utilized by the People's Liberation Army (PLA). Meanwhile, outside naval influences, such as blockade, sanctions, or embargoes, can exert a profound impact on China, just as foreign intervention or, equally important, a decision not to intervene, can often determine the outcome of major maritime events.

Since 1949, two Han Chinese-dominated governments have opposed each other across the Taiwan Strait. Historically, effective rule in China required a strong Mandate of Heaven. Signs of this included the defeat of the ruler's political rivals, the absence of internal rebellions, strong central control over the provinces, and domestic prosperity. As long as the ruler's Mandate of Heaven appeared to be strong, the vast majority of Chinese accepted their fate and would go along with the status quo. If, however, the ruler's Mandate of Heaven seemed questionable, then a new leader might be tempted to claim the mandate for himself while the military could suddenly switch sides in an internal rebellion to abandon the ruling government in favor of its challenger.

In such cases, Han Chinese officials of a deposed dynasty would often shift their loyalties and serve the new dynasty. This was true for the Qing dynasty, the Nationalist government, the Japanese puppet governments of both Manchuria and Mainland China in the 1930s and 1940s, and especially for the Communist government, when entire Nationalist armies defected to serve the Communists. The seventieth anniversary of the founding of the PLA Navy (PLAN) was celebrated on April 23, 2019, which is the date the majority of the Nationalist navy defected to the Communist side.

If the People's Republic of China (PRC) and Taiwan were ever to engage in battle, therefore, it would be Han Chinese on both sides fighting over the perceived legitimacy of a "foreign," USSR-created, Communist dynasty in the PRC versus the "domestic," albeit supported by the United States, Nationalist dynasty on Taiwan. Now that the Nationalist regime has survived on Taiwan for well over sixty years, it may appear to many Chinese that Taiwan's separation from Mainland China is permanent. Cooperation may trump warfare, for example, if the two governments were to form some kind of United Front. However, historical characteristics like Mandate of Heaven could still impact the outcome of any future conflict.

Many Chinese believe they have a Heaven-given right to rule East Asia, similar in some ways with the US view of "manifest destiny" in North America. Until the nineteenth century, when China became engaged with the West, the Chinese believed that the earth had but one civilization ruled by one emperor. The Chinese referred to their land not only as "the Central Kingdom," or *Zhongguo*, but also as *Tianxia*, meaning "all under heaven." All surrounding countries were considered to be tributaries of China and were populated by "barbarians." This tributary-system mentality is still strong in China today. Barbarian management presupposed that China had not only the authority to rule over and regulate the trade and military affairs of the barbarians, but that all intelligent barbarians would naturally seek to emulate Chinese customs.

Over time, the Chinese government developed the tributary system in order to keep the various barbarian groups divided and satisfied, so that they would not gang up against China. The tributary system linked ethnic minorities on the Chinese frontiers to the center via regular tribute missions. It largely insulated China from outside cultural influence by channeling interactions with foreigners within culturally acceptable Chinese norms. The tributary system has often been schematized as a set of concentric circles, with China at the center and ever more barbaric peoples located in the more distant concentric rings surrounding China proper. The near barbarians were Sinified, meaning that they accepted many Han ways, while the more distant barbarians partook of Chinese culture in lesser degrees the further they were from the center. China's Sinified tributaries included Korea, Mongolia, Manchuria, Tibet, Burma, Thailand, and Vietnam, plus island cultures like Taiwan and Okinawa (the Liuqiu or Ryukyu islands). Unsinified tributaries included Tungus peoples of Manchuria and the Uighurs and other Muslim peoples of Central Asia. Later, select European countries, such as Russia, were included in this system as Chinese tributaries.

The tributary relationship was both financial and coercive, including positive and negative incentives. The states that cooperated received lucrative gifts and trade. Those states that did not risked wars of annihilation. China obliterated entire frontier peoples, as occurred during the Qianlong Emperor's conquest of Central Asia in the eighteenth century. Periodically, neighboring barbarian states rebelled against Chinese domination, sometimes to the point of attacking China proper and occasionally even overthrowing the dynasty. The Mongols and Manchus created China's most territorially extensive empires, the Yuan (1264–1368) and Qing (1644–1911) dynasties.

Just as the wielding of military power could propel a Chinese peasant up the vertical ladder to become emperor, tributary peoples could also seize the throne. But the tributary system was meant to prevent this. China employed a strategy of "barbarian management" to deal with uncooperative neighbors. This continental strategy included employing bilateral diplomacy and threats of war to keep its neighbors weak and divided so that they could not unite against China. The Chinese described some of their key barbarian management strategies in four-character idioms: *Yuan jiao jin zheng* means maintaining good relations with the far threat while attacking the near threat. The idiom *yi yi zhi yi* means to use one barbarian to control another, often pitting a more distant group against a closer group. In keeping with these traditions, through until the end of the Maoist era, the Chinese have emphasized bilateral over multilateral relations.

Meanwhile, in relations with foreigners, the concept of "face" was all-important. Face in China is the public perception of a person's worth. Those with face stood far above those without face in Chinese society's steep hierarchy. Face could be maintained, lost, or given. To "have face" meant to acquire public tokens of respect from others. Face could be lost through incompetence, corruption, or meanness in public. So long as these faults remained private, however, there was no loss of face because nobody knew about it. Face was therefore like a zero-sum game, since losing face was something to be feared and avoided. Those at the top of society were more fearful of losing face than those at the bottom. Emperors were no more immune to the fear of loss of face than commoners, in fact more so. Face could also be given. This entailed giving others the public tokens of respect regardless of whether or not they deserved it. Face reflected not reality, but public interpretations of reality, so was highly brittle.

One of the most unique peculiarities in the PLAN is the political commissar system. This system perhaps originated with the Mongol system called military diarchy, where one Mongol commander was paired with a Han Chinese commander. Marco Polo is a good example, since he was hired by the Mongols precisely because he was not Chinese, so owed his allegiance only to the Khan. This dual system was also later adopted by the Qing court, which paired Han and Manchu senior officials. In Russia, which suffered three centuries of Mongol rule, called the Mongol "yoke," the Bolsheviks also utilized the expertise of civil servants and military officers of the former tsarist government, pairing a military expert with a politically reliable Communist called a political commissar.

During the early 1920s, Soviet advisers transformed the Nationalist Party into a highly centralized and disciplined organization, in part by pairing up Communist loyalists with Nationalist experts. Under Mao Zedong the political commissar system embedded Communist party representatives into the structure of the army, which gave the Chinese Communist Party effective control over the army, navy, and air force. One major downside of this system, however, was the potential for poor communications and inefficient coordination, since military officers often mistrusted or even actively opposed their less experienced political commissar.

The 14 case studies in this book will discuss many of these cultural characteristics, while the Conclusions will examine all fourteen case studies together and will try to place them in historical perspective. Do Chinese still worry about "face," and in particular "losing face"? What impact, if any, does the Mandate of Heaven have on modern Chinese? Will Han Chinese on both sides of the Taiwan Strait go to war to determine which "dynasty" should rule all of China? Does the PLAN worry as much about mutiny as earlier dynasties? What is the impact of foreign intervention, foreign decisions not to intervene, and secret diplomacy? Finally, this book will attempt to assess which of these historical characteristics and peculiarities are still present in full-force in China today.

Chapter 1

BATTLE OF BẠCH ĐẰNG RIVER (938)

Chinese views on gaining and losing "face" can play an important role in warfare. In 938, the Vietnamese opposed a fleet sent by the invading southern Han Chinese state called Nan-Han. Ngô Quyền ordered iron-headed poles to be placed under the waters of the Bạch Đằng River, and he then lured the Chinese fleet upriver during high tide. When the tide receded, the enemy's ships were pushed downstream by the strong current and impaled on the poles. Three hundred and fifty years later, in 1288, a Mongol fleet was defeated in exactly the same way in the same place. This suggests that the Han Chinese naval officers did not tell their Mongol commanders about the earlier defeat, either because they did not know about it themselves or, more damning, perhaps considered it a "loss of face" to admit to the Mongols this earlier defeat at the hands of their former tributary, Vietnam.

Summary of the Bạch Đằng River Battle

Sunzi's *Art of War* does not include a single word about sea battles. What he does mention is the importance of currents and, in particular, river currents. Maritime warfare in ancient China was conducted mainly on canals, rivers, and inland lakes, not on the open ocean. River battles could make or break Chinese dynasties. For example, the 663 victory at the mouth of the Paek River was widely considered to be the height of the Tang dynasty's naval activities. Similarly, the 938 defeat at Bạch Đằng River would be the low point of the successor Nan-Han state.

By the eighth and ninth centuries, there was a gradual slowdown of the Tang expansion and a withdrawal from China's far-flung military outposts. Constant wars against the Turks, the Uighurs, the Tibetans, and Arabs in the West drained China's finances. Rebellions meant that large sections of the Tang empire became semi-independent from the capital's control. Finally, in 906, the Tang dynasty fell. China was subdivided into a number of small states, each seeking to dominate the others. While the northern states relied mainly on their large armies, the southern coastal states were maritime powers. This created a military stalemate that lasted for several decades. Nan-Han was one such maritime state, located in modern-day Guangdong province. It became rich through maritime commerce, which allowed it to support a strong navy.

In the midst of this dynastic turmoil, many of the Tang's former tributaries sought greater autonomy, or even full independence, from China. Annam (modern-day Vietnam) had intermittently fallen under Chinese control as early as the reign of Han Wudi (140–87 BCE) and again during the Tang dynasty (618–907). Although the Vietnamese largely adopted the Confucian civil structure and used Chinese characters for writing, there were many notable ethnic and linguistic differences between their culture and the Han Chinese culture.

In 930, the ruler of Nan-Han, Liu Yan, expanded southward by sending a fleet of naval ships to raid Champa, returning with priceless gold and jewels. At this point, the coastal power of Nan-Han extended south to present-day Tongking. In 938, an Annamite named Ngô Quyền, a former Tang officer, rebelled against Nan-Han. Liu Yan sent his navy south to retake the tributary. The Nan-Han fleet was commanded by his son, Liu Hongcao. The fleet left Guangzhou, sailed through the Hainan Straits, and then traveled across the Bay of Tongking to the entrance of the Bạch Đằng River.

Ngô Quyền led his much smaller fleet down river. At high tide, Ngô Quyền sent his lightest ships to attack the Nan-Han fleet. They were quickly defeated and fled back upriver into the Bạch Đằng River. The larger and much heavier Chinese ships gave chase. When the tide began to ebb, however, the bigger Chinese ships could not sail any further. Foiled, they turned around in order to sail back out to sea. However, to their surprise, they soon discovered that iron-tipped stakes made of huge tree trunks were now protruding out of the water, preventing their retreat. It was at this point that Ngô Quyền sent the bulk of his ships back down river to attack, quickly surrounding and destroying most of the Nan-Han ships. Liu Hongcao and over half of his men were slaughtered.

As a result of this victory, Ngô Quyền created an independent Vietnam after a thousand years of being ruled by China. Even today, Vietnamese honor his naval victory as the beginning of modern Vietnamese history. Three hundred years later, General Tran Hung Dao also used wooden poles to defeat a Mongol-led invasion of Vietnam. In honor of this second victory, tourists can still visit the Hang Dau Go (Wooden Poles) cave in Ha Long Bay, where many of the wooden poles were originally stored.

In sharp contrast to the Vietnamese, who gleefully recount stories of their victory over the Han Chinese, it is quite likely that the extreme "loss of face" connected with this defeat meant that the Chinese did not want to dwell on it. This might help explain how the Vietnamese were able to use this exact same tactic again three hundred and fifty years later against the Mongols. Either the Han Chinese advisors to the Mongols were too embarrassed to discuss this earlier defeat, or it is even possible that they did not know about it themselves, having conveniently written it out of their history.

In summary, this critical naval battle on the Bạch Đằng River was important for several reasons. It gained independence for Vietnam after a thousand years of Chinese rule; two years later, Ngô Quyền proclaimed himself king of Annam. It also contributed to the eventual demise of the Nan-Han state. By 960, a new Chinese dynasty, called the Song, was in the process of unifying China, and in 974 the Song navy defeated Nan-Han and incorporated it into the new Song state. Finally, this battle was to have a lasting influence on later naval battles, in particular in 1288 when a Mongol fleet was defeated in almost the exact same place using the same maritime strategy as in 938.

Lessons: There are many important military lessons that can be gained from examining the Bạch Đằng River battle. River battles were more common than conflicts on the high seas. On rivers, the local knowledge of currents and tides was especially important, and the

Vietnamese clearly understood the Bạch Đằng River better than their Chinese adversaries. By sending an inferior force against the Nan-Han fleet, and then retreating upriver, Ngô Quyền was able to lure the Chinese fleet into a trap. Once the trap was sprung, the smaller Vietnamese ships easily defeated their larger Chinese opponents. Finally, and arguably most importantly, some three-hundred-and-fifty years later, the extreme "loss of face" felt by the Chinese apparently allowed this exact same strategy to be equally effective against another Chinese fleet, this time led by the Mongols. Perhaps due to the ethnic difference between the Han admiral and his Mongol co-commander, or due to the Chinese collective memory rewriting history, the lessons of the 938 defeat on the Bạch Đằng River were not passed on to later generations. This oversight resulted in a second historic defeat in 1288 at the hands of the Vietnamese. This type of selective collective memory—that is, ignoring one's defeats and focusing instead only on one's victories—is potentially one important characteristic of the Chinese that can be used by opponents to defeat China in battle.

Chapter 2

BATTLE OF YAISHAN (1279)

The Mandate of Heaven switches from dynasty to dynasty. This transition is often accomplished by civil war. For example, the last remnants of the Song loyalists lost to the Mongols at the Battle of Yaishan on March 19, 1279. Interestingly, both fleets were composed mainly of Han Chinese, and the two Han commanders were born in the same region of North China, shared the same surname, and even belonged to the same clan. The Song supporters hoped to recreate their dynasty while those Han Chinese who fought for the Mongols supported the new Yuan dynasty. After the Yuan victory at Yaishan the Mongols acquired an additional 800 Song ships. As one specialist of the Yuan navy has concluded, it was "essentially the Song navy" fighting itself on both sides of the battle, and that "except for a few thousand Mongols, the Yuan forces that fought at the historic battle of Yaishan were all Han Chinese."[1]

Summary of the Battle of Yaishan

In the first fifty years of the Mongol continental expansion, their armies raided throughout North China, and invaded Russia, Poland, Silesia, Moravia, Hungary, and eastern Austria, eventually pushing south into Asia Minor. But they made little progress against the maritime states of East Asia. For example, for 30 years they were unable to cross the Imjin River to take the island of Kangwha where the Korean king had fled. For 40 years the Mongols maneuvered their forces around the northern and western borders of the Southern

---

[1] Lo Jung-pang, *China as a Sea Power, 1127–1368* (Singapore: NUS Press, 2012), 245–46; much of this section is based on Lo's work.

Song empire, but they were unable to break through the Chinese defensive system between the Huai River and the Yangzi River.[2] All of this changed once Han Chinese defectors knowledgeable about maritime warfare joined the Mongols.

Previously, the Mongols had had little use for boats in their land campaigns. But in 1259, Qubilai Khan promoted Zhang Rongshi to be "Commander of Ten Thousand of the Navy" with the specific goal of training naval officers. In 1265, Qubilai moved his capital to Yanjing, in northern China, and began creating his great capital, Daidu, on the site of modern-day Beijing. Mongol military preparations against the Song included building a navy to penetrate into the waterways of the Chinese defensive system. But despite years of effort, the newly created Yuan navy failed to break through the Song defenses.

In April 1270, a Han Chinese official named Liu Zheng submitted to the Yuan commander-in-chief Aju a memorandum advocating building warships and training sailors in naval warfare. Qubilai approved an edict, dated April 8, 1270, authorizing the construction of 5,000 warships and small-size river boats. Liu Zheng was appointed to supervise training 70,000 sailors, and to conduct daily classes both on ship design and how to handle ships at sea. By fall of 1272, the size of the Yuan fleet had increased to four "wings." Later, four Commanders of Ten Thousand were created, with four wings apiece or a total of 16 wings. On July 20, 1274, Qubilai formally declared war against Song. By December 24, 1274, the first Yuan ships had reached Wuhan at the confluence of the Han and the Yangzi Rivers. By summer 1275, the Yangzi River was firmly under the control of the Mongol forces.

With the end of the riverine phase of the Yuan campaign against the Song, ocean-going ships were now required. This resulted in a year-long delay while sufficient ships and sailors were assembled. Once an ocean-capable navy was ready, the Mongol strategy against the Song capital at Hangzhou was to adopt a three-pronged land–sea drive, two columns to attack by land and the naval force to attack from the sea. Dong Wenbing was appointed to command the Yuan

---

2 Karl Wittfogel, *History of Chinese Society: Liao (907–1125)* (London, Macmillan, 1949), 19.

navy of 780 sea-going ships, mostly of the "Yellow Goose" and "White Falcon" classes with a crew of over ten thousand men. He also sent Wang Shiqiang to persuade Chinese pirates to join the Yuan navy. This added another 500 ships and several thousand experienced seamen to the Yuan fleet. When the Yuan fleet set sail in mid-December 1275, it had a total of 41 wings.

The fleet started moving on December 23, 1275. Sailing down the coast, it reached Zhapu on January 18, 1276, which held out for four days before surrendering. Meanwhile, the two army columns, which had advanced into Zhejiang province separately, met up with the navy a few miles north of Hangzhou on February 3, 1276. After Hangzhou fell, Ataqai and Zhang Hongfan entered the Song capital and escorted the boy emperor and the empress-mother to Bayan's headquarters. On February 10, 1276, with the capitulation of the Song court, the war officially ended. However, two younger brothers of the boy emperor, Prince Guang and Prince Yi, were rescued from the Song capital on a warship commanded by Zhang Shijie, a Song loyalist. On March 25, 1276, they fled south to Fuzhou. On June 14, Prince Guang, age eight, became the new Song emperor. Many Song ships, which had escaped capture or destruction by the Yuan navy, joined them there. After a series of military setbacks, the Song fled further south on December 24, 1276 to Quanzhou (in the West called Zaiton), one of the largest and most prosperous ports in East Asia.

The Yuan–Song naval conflict stalemated for most of 1277. On January 16, 1278, the Han Chinese admiral Liu Shen was patrolling in the waters off the Pearl River when his men sighted a large fleet on the horizon fleeing south. He immediately gave chase, and at the Daya Islands he caught up with the Song ships, capturing 200 ships as well as a number of Song officials. Soon afterward, the child emperor died of a cold and, on May 10, his seven-year old brother Prince Yi became the new Song emperor. The military situation for the Song was dire. Zhang Shijie failed in his attempt to seize a foothold on the Leizhou Peninsula, near Hainan Island. Meanwhile Canton (modern-day Guangzhou), which had revolted for the fifth time, was reoccupied by the Yuan forces.

The Song supporters, totaling 200,000 soldiers and civilians, moved to Yaishan on June 28, 1278. The new base was a small island protected in the north and the east by mud flats, which were virtually impassable on foot. On its west and south, there was a 14-mile-long and two-and-a-half-mile-wide lagoon. The entrance to the lagoon was a mile-wide channel overlooked by towering hills. Seeing that the lagoon was large enough to accommodate his entire fleet, Zhang Shijie considered Yaishan an ideal location for his base. After arriving, his men chopped trees from the hillside to build 30 large buildings to serve as the palace of the emperor, and smaller huts were built to serve as barracks. The construction and repair of ships, and making weapons, lasted until November 1278.

On February 14, 1279, the main Yuan fleet under Zhang Hongfan set sail, while on February 28, a second Han Chinese official named Li Heng left Canton with 120 ships under his command. On March 6, the two Yuan fleets met outside the entrance of Yaishan. The next morning, Zhang Hongfan ordered a preliminary attack. Zhang Shijie was ready. He knew that his men had low morale, and might flee. So he said, "We have been at sea for years. When will it end? This is the time to fight and to decide on victory or defeat." He ordered the buildings to be burnt and everybody moved onboard the ships, which he ordered to be lashed together.[3] This put his men on "death ground," forcing them to fight harder.

The details of the battle around Yaishan were described in two contemporary works: the official records of the Yuan government and an eyewitness story by a historian on board the Song fleet. According to these accounts, Commander-in-chief Zhang Hongfan only had 500 ships, but they were extremely mobile. By contrast, Zhang Shijie put over a thousand of his ships in a straight line, lashed together with ropes, and with ramparts built for self-protection. On all four sides there were turreted ships, like towers in a fortified city. The Chinese ships were coated with mud to protect them against fireships, and they were equipped with bamboo tubes full of water. In the center of the fleet, a large vessel served as the "palace" of the imperial family.

Strategically, the Song fortifications looked impressive. Not only could an attacking force approach only by water, but Zhang Shijie was ready to repel a variety of attacks, including fireships. Tactically, however, the Song position was actually quite poor. Since the land was left undefended, the Song leader intentionally ceded his main

---

3 *Sung Shih*, ch. 451, 7; cited by Lo, *China as a Sea Power*.

resource base to the Yuan troops, again to force his men to fight harder by putting them on "death ground." But shortages of firewood and fresh water soon reduced the defenders to slow starvation. This put time on the side of the attackers, not the defenders.

The Yuan forces made the first move. Zhang Hongfan ordered two junior officers to begin to make diversionary attacks on the enemy from the west and from the south, while he and Li Heng directed the main assaults on the northwest and southwest corners where the enemy could not concentrate the full force of his artillery fire. The final battle began on March 19, and lasted from 9:00 a.m. to almost 5:00 p.m. Near the end of the day the Yuan forces gained a strategic advantage and the Song became disheartened and demoralized. Many Song jumped into the sea and drowned.

When Zhang Shijie realized the battle was lost, he ordered the withdrawal of the final Song troops to the center. Zhang decided to fight his way out of the harbor, but he needed to find the emperor first. He sent a boat to collect the Emperor Yi, but the guards thought it was an enemy boat sent as a trick and refused to let him go; later, the emperor was drowned by his own guards to ensure that he would not be captured by the Mongols. Zhang Shijie waited as long as he could, but when the boat did not return, he and his men boarded 16 large ships, chopped the ropes that bound them to the other vessels, and fought their way out of the lagoon entrance.

As soon as Zhang Hongfan and Li Heng discovered that many Song ships were escaping, they immediately chased them. When they reached the entrance to the lagoon, however, the smoke and fog was so thick that the Yuan commanders lost sight of the escaping Song ships. Zhang Shijie sailed to Annam, but his ship was wrecked on June 14, 1279. However, many of his officers and men survived and fled to Indochina. There is no indication that they ever returned to China.

The Yuan navy had won a great naval victory, destroying the last fleet of the Song navy. It acquired 800 warships, not counting the vessels that were sunk and burnt. Over a hundred thousand Song were reportedly killed or captured. Zhang Hongfan left Yaishan six days after the battle. Before his departure, he ordered his men to carve on a rock that towered above the channel entrance the inscription: "Zhang Hongfan destroyed the Sung here."

By backing the Mongols and assisting them to destroy the Song dynasty, Zhang Hongfan was later denounced as a traitor. After all, Zhang Hongfan was a native of North China, born not far from the birthplace of his clansman and opponent, Zhang Shijie. Except for a few thousand Mongols, the Yuan forces that fought at the battle of Yaishan were all Han Chinese. This emphasizes the fact that the Yuan navy was not only patterned after the Song navy but also used captured Song ships and their crews, and exploited Song maritime experience and technology. Furthermore, the guiding generals were almost all Chinese, from Liu Zheng who promoted the expansion of the navy to Zhang Hongfan, whose victory at Yaishan climaxed the rise of the Yuan navy. Without the assistance of the Han Chinese, the Mongols would have had a difficult, if not impossible, task of building a navy and in conquering South China. In retrospect, the Yuan navy was essentially the Song navy flying a new flag.

Lesson: Following the widespread perception that the Mandate of Heaven had shifted from the Song to the Yuan dynasty, Han Chinese soldiers and sailors carried out most of the fighting on both sides of the Yaishan battle. The two opposing admirals at the Battle of Yaishan had the same family name and clan, were born in the same district in northern China, and yet one fought for the Song and the other for the Yuan. In many ways the current stalemate along the Taiwan Strait parallels this historic battle, as Han Chinese fighting for the "Communist" dynasty in Mainland China are pitted against those supporting the "Nationalist" dynasty in Taiwan. Similar to the Yuan–Song conflict, the Communists are a land-based northern-based government fighting a naval opponent located in the south. Finally, if one thinks of Communism as coming to China from the Soviet Union, then there is an outward appearance of an alien conquest—similar to the Mongols—fighting a more indigenous Han Chinese nationalist movement.

Chapter 3
BATTLE OF LAKE POYANG (1363)

Small navies can often defeat large ones. Before the Ming dynasty could overthrow Mongol rule in China, it first had to defeat the other Han Chinese states rivaling it for power. The main battlefield was not on a river or at sea but was on one of China's largest fresh water lakes. The battle of Lake Poyang was fought from August 30–October 4, 1363 in Jiangxi province. The Ming fleet separated into squadrons, with the heavier ships at the center, and made a frontal assault on the Han ships. The Ming ships were lighter and smaller compared to the Han ships. By using fireships many Han ships were either damaged or destroyed. The Ming then blockaded the Han fleet for a month. On October 4, the final battle began. The Ming again employed fireships. In the midst of fighting, the Han leader Chen Youliang was killed, and the Han surrendered. The Ming victory unified opposition to the Mongols, which five years later resulted in the collapse of the Yuan dynasty in 1368.

Summary of the Battle of Lake Poyang

The Battle of Lake Poyang illustrates that a navy's size is not the only factor in warfare. Described as one of the largest naval battles in world history up until this time, this conflict pitted Zhu Yuanzhang, the founder of the Ming dynasty, against the Han state commander Chen Youliang. At this point, the Mongols continued to rule China as the Yuan dynasty. A number of Han Chinese breakaway states, however, sought to consolidate resistance to the Mongols. The crucial battle occurred on Poyang Lake, the largest Chinese freshwater lake at that time, located in Jiangxi province just south of the Yangzi River.

The Han state initiated fighting when it attacked Nanchang, which was under the control of the Ming state. When the city resisted, fighting on Lake Poyang became the main focus of the conflict. The Ming fleet was made up of many small ships divided into 11 squadrons, while the Han fleet was composed of large ships (known as "tower ships" or *lou chuan*). While normally the larger fleet could easily dominate the smaller one, the water in Lake Poyang was at its normally low seasonal level, which allowed the smaller and more nimble ships to dominate fighting in shallow waters.

Fighting began on August 30, 1363 when the Ming attacked the Han fleet with fireships, setting twenty *lou chuan* on fire. The smaller Ming ships then tried to surround and board the tower ships, but failed. Zhu's flagship narrowly escaped being captured. Fighting resumed the next day, on August 31. This time the Han ships were arranged in a solid line held together by chains. Fireships were used again, and due to a favorable wind, they worked well against the mass of enemy ships. Many of the tower ships being used by the Han were destroyed or damaged, but the outcome of the battle was inconclusive.

After a delay of two days, fighting resumed on September 2. This time, Commander Chen Youliang arranged his large ships in a more open formation, which unintentionally proved advantageous to the Ming, who could use the resulting openings to more easily board individual ships. For the next month the two fleets continued to fight, but neither navy gained a decisive advantage. Since neither side wanted to engage in a war of attrition, perhaps more concerned about their mutual enemy the Mongols, they were each cautious about expending forces unnecessarily.

This situation suddenly changed on October 4, when the Ming employed fireships once again, this time with greater effect. In the midst of battle Chen Youliang was killed by a stray arrow to the head, prompting the Han to surrender shortly afterward. The Ming victory at the Lake Poyang battle was critical in forming a unified Han Chinese resistance against the Mongols. In 1368, Zhu Yuanzhang's forces defeated the Mongols, and Zhu became the Ming dynasty's founding Hongwu emperor.

Lesson: The larger fleet with the bigger ships does not always win in Chinese naval battles. In the case of the Lake Poyang battle, the smaller Ming ships were able to use fireships effectively and they could also surround and board the larger Han ships, thereby destroying them sequentially. The death of Chen Youliang demoralized the Han, leading to their surrender. Over five-hundred years later, a similarly counterintuitive outcome would occur in 1894 during the Battle of the Yellow Sea, when Admiral Ding Ruchang was wounded and the smaller but faster Japanese fleet was able to outflank and defeat the much larger Chinese fleet. In the current standoff between China and Japan over the East China Sea, and among China, Taiwan, Vietnam, the Philippines, Malaysia, Brunei, and Indonesia over control of the islands in the South China Sea, it should not be taken for granted that China's larger navy will succeed. History has shown that a large Chinese force can be defeated by a smaller force, in particular if it employs a superior strategy and can maximize its military advantages, such as greater speed, better weapons, and a higher degree of jointness.

Chapter 4

MING–KOTTE WAR IN SOUTHEAST ASIA (1410–11)

The Chinese navy has often been tasked to carry out expansionist policies. Admiral Zheng He is usually credited for commanding seven peaceful naval missions during the Ming dynasty to explore and set up trade with China's southern neighbors. However, in 1410, a Chinese fleet arrived in local waters near Sri Lanka seeking to establish Chinese power along the local maritime routes. When pirates, supported by the Kotte King Alakeshvara, attacked the Chinese ships a conflict broke out in southern Sri Lanka. During the Ming–Kotte war (1410–11), Admiral Zheng He and his troops invaded Kotte, conquered its capital, took its king and his family hostage, and brought them back to China. Eventually, the Yongle Emperor freed Alakeshvara, but when he got home a new pro-Chinese king had already taken the throne. Future Sri Lankan tribute missions to Beijing pledged their loyalty as part of China's extended tributary system. With Chinese power secured, Kotte pirates never again bothered a Ming treasure fleet.

Summary of the Ming–Kotte War

During the early years of the Ming dynasty, a deep-sea armada under Admiral Zheng He set sail in 1405 for a two-year voyage to the South China Sea and the Indian Ocean. In a total of seven expeditions that continued through 1433, these Chinese fleets visited Cochin, Siam, Java, Malacca, Sri Lanka, India, the Persian Gulf, and perhaps traveled as far south and west as southern Africa.[1] Zheng He set up

---

1 Louise Levathes, *When China Ruled the Seas: The Treasure Fleet of the Dragon Throne, 1405–1433* (New York: Oxford University Press, 1994).

several strategic bases and trading centers during these voyages, most notably at Malacca, just up the Malaysian coastline from modern-day Singapore. As a result of his travels, many rare delicacies and strange animals were brought back to China.

These voyages are generally portrayed by the Chinese as peaceful. However, the Ming also used these voyages to claim land for China and to dominate local governments, which undermines descriptions of the voyages as nonmilitary expeditions. These early visits during the Ming, and claims that Chinese fishermen and fishing vessels were present in South China Sea waters for hundreds of years, have been used to date Chinese sovereignty over these disputed islands all the way back to the fifteenth century. Later, Communist historians argued that Zheng He stopped at the Paracel and Spratly Islands on his voyages, thus proving Chinese sovereignty there.

China's riverine and sea-going navy was clearly superior in both size and technological development to the Southeast Asian navies. Admiral Zheng He arrived off Sri Lanka intent on establishing Chinese control of the maritime routes in the Indian Ocean. King Alakeshvara of the Kotte kingdom was accused of supporting pirates who interfered with the Chinese trade. During the third treasure voyage, King Alakeshvara reportedly planned to launch a surprise attack on the fleet. Zheng He and approximately two thousand Ming troops traveled overland into Kotte, conquered the capital, and took Alakeshvara, his family, and principal officials captive. Zheng He returned to Nanjing on July 6, 1411 and presented his prisoners to the Yongle Emperor. Later, Alakeshvara was freed, but by the time he returned to Sri Lanka a new, more pro-Chinese, king was on the throne.

Zheng He's voyages are usually portrayed by Chinese authors as sponsoring "peace and friendship" with countries in South and Southeast Asia, but the Ming–Kotte War was a particularly clear example of Chinese imperialism. As one scholar has explained, the "military invasion of Sri Lanka" was perhaps the "most telling as to the nature of the eunuch-led maritime voyages." Not only was the local ruler overthrown and his army destroyed but a pro-Chinese "puppet ruler" was put on the throne. The Ming court rewarded the troops for their victory, and the simple fact that they "were rewarded in the same manner and at equivalent levels to those forces which invaded Dai Viet [Vietnam] in 1406" suggested that the two events had "similar aims."[2]

Chinese treasure fleets and exploration was curtailed after the seventh voyage. One possible reason was that in 1418, Annam erupted in revolution, which imperiled the sea lanes off Vietnam's coastline. By 1427, the Annamese had reclaimed their independence from China and so had cut off the normally secure maritime route along Vietnam's coast. Loss of the Chinese tributary in Annam put serious limits on the viability of Zheng He's expeditions, which ended only a few years later. These events show that Chinese imperialism did not continue unopposed. To carry out further voyages to Malacca would have required first conducting additional military campaigns in Annam. Later, Ming bureaucrats who opposed plans to fund a new series of overseas voyages reportedly destroyed most of the navigation records from Zheng He's earlier voyages. The deliberate purging of all relevant documents has perhaps obscured the imperialist nature of these undertakings.

Lesson: China has long been a continental empire, but also adopted imperialist policies with regard to its maritime neighbors. To expand its empire to the south China has used expeditionary warfare in Southeast Asia for over five-hundred years. The story of the Ming–Kotte war challenges claims that the Ming treasure fleets were entirely peaceful. In fact, China's relations with its southern neighbors have never been overfriendly. While not full colonies in the Western sense of the term, the "maritime proto-colonialism" carried out by Zheng He "involved the use of huge military force to invade peoples who were ethnically different from the Chinese, to occupy their territory, to break the territory into smaller administrative units, to appoint pliant rulers and 'advisers', and to economically exploit the regions so occupied."[3] Historically, Chinese relations with its southern neighbors have been particularly tense. Disputes over the various island chains

---

2 Geoff Wade, "The Zheng He Voyages: A Reassessment," *Journal of the Malaysian Branch of the Royal Asiatic Society* 78, 1 (2005), 37–58; 49–50.
3 Ibid., 55.

in the South China Sea continue to this day. Many of the countries in that region oppose China's most recent island-building policies, knowing full well the consequences of Chinese imperialism on their own states. Interestingly, Sri Lanka has not been one of them, and the PRC has invested billions of dollars in port facilities there and has just agreed to construct a train line to service it.

Chapter 5

MING LOYALISTS FLEE TO TAIWAN (1661–83)

Offshore islands have played an important political and military role throughout Chinese history. During the mid-to-late seventeenth century, Ming loyalist Zheng Chenggong opposed the Manchu invasion of China, which resulted in the creation of the Qing dynasty in 1644. Retreating to Taiwan, Zheng defeated the Dutch, who had taken the island in 1624, at Zeelandia in 1661. When Zheng died in 1662, his followers continued their opposition to the Qing from Taiwan. While Zheng is condemned in Qing dynasty sources for opposing the central government of China, in Communist sources he is lauded for expelling the Dutch. This shows how contradictory certain events are viewed in Chinese history.

Summary of the Ming Opposition on Taiwan

Near the end of the Ming dynasty, Taiwan became the venue for naval conflict. During the 1620s, a new trading power, the Dutch, based themselves in Taiwan, which they called *Formosa* (meaning "Beautiful island" in Portuguese). Following the collapse of the Ming dynasty in 1644, the Manchu Qing dynasty dominated northern China and slowly moved southward. The Manchus were opposed by Zheng Chenggong (1624–62), better known in Western studies as Koxinga, which came from his Ming title "Lord of the Imperial Surname," which in Chinese transliteration reads as "Guo Xing Ye."

Zheng Chenggong had a Japanese mother, but a Chinese father, who was one of the leaders of the so-called Japanese pirates, or *wokou*. Joining the Han Chinese against the invading Manchus, Zheng became a Ming loyalist. In 1659, he became famous for leading a maritime expedition of more than 100,000 troops up the Yangzi River to attack the Qing's southern headquarters at Nanjing. This attack failed. However, Zheng is best known for reestablishing Chinese control over Taiwan: in April 1661, Zheng's 25,000 forces landed near the Dutch stronghold at Anping, the modern-day city of Tainan. After a nine-month siege, the fortress of Zeelandia capitulated. Zheng allowed the Dutch to leave unharmed in return for acquiring their claim over Taiwan.

Zheng Chenggong holds a rather unique place in the history of Chinese coastal defense, since he was simultaneously considered to be a Japanese pirate, an anti-Manchu Ming loyalist, and a Han nationalist credited with ousting the Dutch and reasserting Chinese control over Taiwan. Zheng is variously described by contemporary PRC sources as a "patriotic general," a "Chinese national hero," and as a military leader who "commanded landing operations to expel the Dutch colonizers and recover Taiwan."[1] The fact that Zheng spent most of his career opposing the central Chinese government is largely overlooked or forgiven by the PRC.

Zheng Chenggong's theories of how to retake Taiwan are still studied by contemporary PLAN officers. His strategy to retake Taiwan has been divided into four parts. First, after recognizing the strategic value of Taiwan to fight the Manchus, he advocated taking control of Jinmen (Quemoy) and other offshore islands as an advanced base to assault the Dutch stronghold on Taiwan, stating, "Clear away a thorny path to drive out the barbarians." Second, he emphasized a strong navy and the strict training of an elite army of crack troops. Third, after assaulting and taking control of the Penghu Islands (Pescadores), his navy would "surround and annihilate" the enemy's ships, thus pinning the enemy in their strongholds. Zheng's troops would then invade at Luermen, a small port in southern Taiwan; convince the native followers of the Dutch to revolt; and then attack the enemy's fortress at Anping. Fourth, after achieving military victory,

---

1 "Zheng Chenggong shoufu Taiwan junshi lunshu" (Zheng Chenggong's military views of recapturing Taiwan) and "Zheng Chenggong shoufu Taiwan zhi zhan" (Zheng Chenggong, Operation for Recapturing Taiwan by) in *Zhongguo Haijun Baike Quanshu* (*Chinese Naval Encyclopedia*), Vol. II, 1912–14.

Zheng would "abolish the colonial system founded by the Dutch" and establish his own anti-Manchu government over Taiwan.[2]

Zheng followed his military success over the Dutch by establishing an opposition government in Taiwan and basing his troops there. He also supported a massive program of Han Chinese immigration from Fujian province to Taiwan; many of today's Taiwanese can trace their family line back to this exodus. Although Zheng intended to continue his anti-Manchu offensive from Taiwan, he died on June 23, 1662. Zheng's successors held out against the Qing rulers another twenty years. In 1683, a Qing fleet under Admiral Shi Lang took Taiwan back by force. This military expedition returned Taiwan to Chinese rule after an almost 60-year absence. The timing of this event is quite important. Counting from 1624, the Qing took back Taiwan immediately prior to its 60th year of separation from China. Sixty is a particularly important year in China's sexagenary cycle, since once a situation has existed unchanged for sixty years it is usually considered permanent. For example, the continued existence of a separatist Taiwan for 70 years (from 1949 to 2019) suggests to some that it is now a permanent state.

Lesson: Offshore islands can have great strategic value. The seventeenth-century pirate Zheng Chenggong used offshore islands in the Taiwan Strait like Jinmen to invade Taiwan. In April 1661, Zheng's 25,000 troops launched their attack against the Dutch from the Penghu Islands. After a lengthy siege, Zheng took control of Taiwan. Zheng is honored by contemporary Chinese sources for expelling the Dutch from Taiwan. Since that time, Taiwan has repeatedly been used as a sanctuary for the losing side in Chinese civil wars, including since 1949 by the Nationalist government in exile. Similar to Zheng, Chiang Kai-shek is lauded by the PRC for defeating Japan in World War II, but at the same time vilified for fleeing to Taiwan so as to continue fighting Communism. The current conflict in the South China Sea over a number of small islands, some only inches above the high tide mark, reflects Chinese historical beliefs that offshore islands can be used both as bastions for defense and forward positions for offense. Since the PRC and Taiwan agree these waters are China's, there is always a chance they will cooperate against the other regional claimants.

---

2 Ibid.

Chapter 6

BATTLE OF CHUANBI (1839)

Manchu versus Han tensions often resulted in military defeat at foreign hands. One of the strangest encounters between the British and Chinese during the first Opium War was the Battle of Chuanbi. On November 3, 1839, *Volage* and *Hyacinth* faced off and defeated 16 Han Chinese-manned war junks attempting to defend a foreign merchant ship that had signed the Manchu anti-opium pledge. Unlike the rather ambiguous results of an earlier encounter, in this naval battle the two British sailing ships used their maneuverability before the wind to "slip and cut" among the slower Chinese junks, all the while "delivering broadsides as they ran."[1] In the end the Royal Navy defeated the Qing by blockading the Yangzi River, thus threatening to starve out the Manchu court in Beijing. Han Chinese merchants in the South mainly profited from this victory. PRC historians agree that the Manchus were bad rulers, but still condemn the British for winning the Opium Wars rather than portraying the conflicts as a joint Han–British victory over the Manchus.

Summary of the Battle of Chuanbi

In September 1836, the Qing Emperor, Daoguang, ordered the governor-general in Guangzhou to eliminate all opium imports. China had initially prohibited the smoking of opium in 1729, and had then outlawed its growth and importation in 1796, but these laws were never enforced. As a result, there was a large domestic opium trade in China. By the 1830s, millions of dollars in silver were also being shipped out of China every year, primarily by British traders

---

1 Brian Inglis, *The Opium War* (London: Hodder and Stoughton, 1976), 178–79.

in return for the importation of high-quality Indian opium. So long as China retained a foreign trade surplus, the Qing emperors had ignored opium imports. But once the silver drain became too severe, their decision to ban foreign opium suddenly became a top priority.

For a time, the Qing government toyed with legalizing opium imports and imposing a tariff similar to other foreign medicines. But, this solution would strengthen not weaken the already wealthy Han Chinese merchant class in South China, who sought greater autonomy from Beijing. Domestic Han–Manchu tensions perhaps convinced the Daoguang Emperor to "kill two birds with one stone," by trying to eliminate at one stroke both the foreign threat—the opium traders—and the domestic threat—Han Chinese merchants.

In late 1838, the Daoguang Emperor assigned Lin Zexu, a Han Chinese official, to be the high commissioner of Guangzhou and ordered him to end the opium trade. Chinese Communist authors have quixotically lauded Commissioner Lin, who was a Han Chinese official loyal to the Manchus, as a "patriotic comrade" and a "people's hero."[2] Similar to Communist views of Zheng Chenggong, this is a clear contradiction, since one of Lin's primary tasks was to support the Manchu invaders of China to undermine the power of the southern merchants, who were primarily Han Chinese.

Lin also assumed military command over the Guangdong Navy, since he was simultaneously ordered "to investigate port affairs," to stop smuggling.[3] Pitting one Han Chinese loyal to an alien emperor against other Han Chinese merchants parallels Zhang Hongfan's victory over the Song forces at Yaishan. But Lin soon realized the superiority of the foreign ships, and so sought to avoid direct military conflict. Instead, Lin hoped to use traditional coastal defense strategies against the British, including trade bans, moving coastal populations inland, enhancing coastal and river defenses, bribing recalcitrants with wealth or rank or, finally, the use of diplomacy. If

---

2 Yao Wei-yüan and Hsiao Chih-chih, eds., *Ya-p'ien chan-cheng yen-chiu* (Wu-ch'ang: Wu-han Ta-hsüeh ch'u-pan-she, 1987), 255–58.
3 Edgar Holt, *The Opium Wars in China* (Chester Springs, PA: Dufour Editions, 1964), 78.

everything else failed, China could grant temporary trade privileges to bribe foreign powers into submitting to their will.[4]

On February 26, 1839, Lin attempted to reassert control over both the Han Chinese merchants and the foreign traders by executing a Chinese opium smuggler in front of the foreign-run factories in Guangzhou. In March 1839, Lin ordered the foreigners to hand over all of their stocks of opium, as well as sign a pledge never to trade in opium again. By signing this pledge, the foreign merchants tacitly made themselves subject to Chinese law, which the British government did not trust. When the foreigners refused, on March 24, Lin ordered the blockade of the foreign factories. Chinese workers were told to stay away, and all entrances to the foreign area were barricaded.

On March 27, Charles Elliot, the British chief superintendent, ordered the British traders to turn over all foreign-owned opium chests to him, after which he would give them to Lin. This made these events a state-to-state matter. The Chinese government was now directly responsible to the British government for restitution. Chinese officials, however, interpreted Elliot's decision to hand over the opium as a full retreat. Commissioner Lin proclaimed victory. Under Lin's supervision, the Chinese confiscated and destroyed over twenty thousand cases of opium. With their factories blockaded, the British merchants retreated to one of the offshore islands not far from the mouth of the Pearl River. By July 1839, there were an estimated 50 British ships anchored in a protected bay near the island of Hong Kong.

Superintendent Elliot blamed Commissioner Lin for threatening the British, stating that for "the first time, in our intercourse with this Empire, its government has taken the unprovoked initiative in aggressive measures against British life, liberty, and property, and against the dignity of the Crown."[5] By handing over the opium himself, Elliot made the chests British property. This in turn made the Chinese government liable directly to the British Crown for all losses.

---

4 Bruce Swanson, *Eighth Voyage of the Dragon: A History of China's Quest for Seapower* (Annapolis, MD: Naval Institute Press, 1982), 56.
5 Inglis, *The Opium War*, 120.

Lord Palmerston himself wrote to Elliot informing him that a British expeditionary force would be sent to deal with China.

This situation remained tense through early July 1839, when British sailors on shore leave got in a dispute and ended up murdering a Chinese man. In response, Lin ordered local Chinese merchants not to sell supplies to the British. He reportedly also ordered that all local springs near Hong Kong be poisoned so as to deprive the British of potable water. On August 25, Captain Elliot protested directly to Lin that the Chinese decision to blockade the British left them no choice but to take what they needed by force. Thus, what to most appeared to be a minor incident over access to supplies soon escalated into war.

The opening shot in the first Opium War, called the "Battle of Kowloon," occurred on September 4, 1839, when Captain Elliot led a small fleet of ships to the town of Kowloon, right across from Hong Kong, to demand food and fresh water. When these were not forthcoming, he ordered an attack on the Chinese junks protecting the town. In this naval encounter, Elliot's three ships—the cutters *Louisa* and *Pearl*, supported by the pinnace from *Volage*—faced a number of Chinese war junks. After *Louisa* had fired 104 rounds, it began to run low on ammunition. Elliot ordered the British ships to retreat. Lin was convinced that the Chinese forces had won, even writing the Daoguang Emperor in Beijing to report the exaggerated news that one British vessel had been sunk and many foreign sailors killed. This event became the first victory in what would eventually be described as the "six smashing blows."

When the Chinese fleet saw action a second time on November 3, 1839, however, at the Battle of Chuanbi, the one-sided results should have been clear to Lin. The British ship *Royal Saxon*, which had signed the Manchu pledge promising not to sell opium, tried to enter Guangzhou against the orders of the Superintendent Elliot. When the British ship *Volage* tried to stop the British merchant ship by shooting across her bow, several Han Chinese-manned junks interfered to defend the merchant ship. Thus, "Chinese junks staffed by Han sailors [were] fighting to protect a British ship that had signed the Manchu's anti-opium bond from other British ships trying to stop her entering port."[6]

---

6 Bruce A. Elleman, *Modern Chinese Warfare, 1795–1989* (London: Routledge Press, 2001), 19.

The battle was one-sided, largely due to the British ship's superior technology, but perhaps also partly due to the fact that the Han Chinese sailors had no interest in supporting the Manchus. According to one description of the battle, "Three more junks went down. Several others were deserted by their terrified crews. The rest tried to run—all except the admiral's flagship which, mounting the unusual total of twelve guns, and with the admiral himself erect before the single, immense mast, continued to stand against the English though she had been holed repeatedly and was on the point of foundering."[7]

Britain's naval victory proved that its more modern ships, which were specifically designed to travel on the high seas, could easily out-maneuver, out-flank, and out-gun its Chinese counterparts. The adoption of copper sheathing at the end of the eighteenth century meant that British ships could spend months at sea without repair. Medical advances to cope with scurvy and other illnesses allowed British crews to remain healthy even after extended voyages at sea. Finally, by basing their ships in the relative security of the offshore islands, such as the island of Hong Kong near Guangzhou, and later at the island of Dinghai further to the north near Shanghai, the British fleet remained largely invulnerable from attack.

Following this naval victory, a British contingent cruised northward to threaten Beijing. The Emperor, shocked that the foreigners were on his very doorstep, agreed to negotiations with the British, and a temporary measure was signed. The Qing hoped that by blockading the offshore islands the British would eventually be forced into retreat. What they did not foresee was that the British logistical lines ran all the way back to India, and from there to England. The Chinese could not starve the British out, nor could Chinese ships successfully challenge the British ships one-on-one. British forces eventually retaliated by invading the Yangzi River and blockading access to Grand Canal, thus cutting supplies to Beijing; the Manchu emperor had no choice but to capitulate. As a result of China's defeat, Qing officials like Lin realized that Chinese junks were simply no match for the British vessels. This led to China's earliest advocates for modernizing its naval forces so as to meet force with force.

---

7 Inglis, *The Opium War*, 178–79.

Lesson: Manchu versus Han tensions helped the British defeat China. Given the mix of races and the goals of foreign intervention, events in China are often more complicated than they might at first appear. Chinese histories tend to overlook that Lin Zexu was a Han Chinese official working for the Manchus against the economic interests of the South Chinese merchants. Many Han Chinese merchants undoubtedly supported the British traders against their own "barbarian" government. Using the British to defeat the Manchus is a clear case of "using one barbarian to control another." After World War II, Chiang Kai-shek similarly tried, but failed, to play the United States off the Communist government in Beijing, which was portrayed in Nationalist propaganda as little more than a puppet of another northern "barbarian" invader, the USSR.

Chapter 7

SINO-FRENCH WAR (1884–85)

Regionalism in China can easily result in military defeat. On August 23, 1884, a French fleet under Admiral Courbet entered Fuzhou Harbor and attacked the Nanyang fleet. In a matter of hours it sank nine of the eleven modern Chinese-built ships while they were still in port. When the south requested assistance from China's northern navy, called the Beiyang fleet, Li Hongzhang, the Viceroy of Zhili province, refused to place his own ships in danger, which guaranteed that France could dominate China's southern coastal waters. In the end, China was forced to sue for peace and accept France's terms, which included granting Vietnam its independence from China. The stripping away of a major tributary state like Vietnam was a crucial step in the incremental dismemberment of the Chinese empire.

Summary of Chinese Tensions with France

The Sino-French war was fought over French control of Annam (Vietnam), an on-again off-again Chinese tributary state from the Han dynasty onward. The French hoped to split Annam away from China and make it a French protectorate. China possessed a modern navy—on paper at least—by the early 1880s, but it was not a united and well-coordinated force. While its four fleets possessed a variety of modern ships, each fleet was designed to defend only its specific region, and so refused to come to another fleet's aid. Although the impact of regionalism may appear slight in peacetime, it can make all of the difference during periods of warfare.

One of the most important Chinese naval bases during the early 1870s was at the Fuzhou shipyards. On August 23, 1884, a French fleet of eight ships under Admiral Courbet conducted a surprise attack against the southern fleet's base at Fuzhou. The French fleet destroyed all but two of the eleven modern Chinese-built ships while they were still anchored at port. Within the space of less than one hour, naval bombardments destroyed not only the cream of China's southern fleet but also the Fuzhou shipyard, which had been built with French aid beginning in 1866.[1] Approximately three thousand Chinese were killed, and damage to ships and docks were estimated at USD 15 million.[2]

John Rawlinson has discussed this naval battle at some length and has concluded that the "French advantage was not overwhelming" and that "had they been decisive, the Chinese might have seized a last opportunity." The French took advantage of the swift tides in Mawei Harbor to move quickly upstream against the Chinese ships, which were crowded together close to the docks. Beginning with the deployment of their torpedo boats, the French then used their heavy 10-inch guns to destroy first the Chinese fleet, and secondarily the neighboring dockyards.[3] The destruction of the Chinese fleet and the Fuzhou dockyards was soon complete.

Although the South requested assistance on numerous occasions from the northern fleet, Viceroy Li refused to send the Beiyang fleet to help. In addition, ships from the Guangzhou fleet made it clear that "Canton was not in the war—this being simply a local dispute—they held completely aloof from us." The notable absence of China's Beiyang and Guangzhou fleets from the war virtually guaranteed that the French forces would dominate China's southern coastal waters. As Benjamin A. Elman has concluded, China's defeat was mainly due to "the lack of coordination between the vulnerable Chinese fleet based at the Fuzhou Shipyard and the Beiyang Fleet under Li Hongzhang's

---

1 This French surprise attack against a fleet in port was later copied by Japan's navy both at Port Arthur in 1894 and 1904, and then much later at Pearl Harbor in 1941.
2 Lloyd E. Eastman, *Throne and Mandarins: China's Search for a Policy during the Sino-French Controversy* (Cambridge, MA: Harvard University Press, 1967), 155–56.
3 John L. Rawlinson, *China's Struggle for Naval Development, 1839–1895* (Cambridge, MA: Harvard University Press, 1967), 116–20.

control in the north."⁴ One foreign observer even noted humorously that southern warships would anchor next to the Nanyang fleet at night for protection, but only with the clear understanding that they would not fight if that fleet was attacked by the French.

The Qing Emperor assigned Li Hongzhang to open peace talks with the French. In the final round, Li was negotiating with France's new minister to China, Jules Patenôtre. On June 9, 1885, a Sino-French peace treaty was signed in Tianjin. As a result, Annam became a French protectorate and the Annamese government was forced to conduct its foreign relations solely through France. Over time, France used its position of strength to turn Annam (later-day Vietnam) into a full colony.

Lesson: Regional loyalties, a focus on provincial defense rather than national defense, and political distrust among the different naval fleets greatly facilitated France's victory over China. The Manchus tried to modernize the Chinese navy, but when faced with a foreign threat the regional fleets refused to support each other. The Sino-French war of 1884–85 can be seen as China's first failure of its newly modernized navy, mainly due to a lack of jointness. Regional tensions still exist throughout the PRC that can easily undermine jointness. For example, during the 2001 EP-3 negotiations, US diplomats were reportedly told by Beijing that they had to work not just with the capital but directly with the local authorities on Hainan Island to obtain the release of the American crew.

---

4 Benjamin A. Elman, "Naval Warfare and the Refraction of China's Self-Strengthening Reforms into Scientific and Technological Failure, 1865–1895," *Modern Asian Studies* 38, 2 (2004) 283–326, 316.

Chapter 8

QING BEIYANG FLEET'S DEFEAT IN THE BATTLE OF THE YELLOW SEA (1894)

The proper adaption and efficient use of Western naval equipment has been a constant challenge to China. In the opening days of the first Sino-Japanese War, foreigners were convinced that China would win. Two of its German-made ships had such thick armor that the Japanese guns could not pierce them. During September 1894, however, the Japanese defeated China in the Battle of the Yellow Sea (also called the Battle of the Yalu). Not only did the Chinese ships have inadequate ammunition, and so quickly ran out, but putting the heavier ships in the center to protect them allowed the Japanese to pick off the older and weaker ships on the wings, thus easily winning the battle.

Summary of the 1894–95 Sino-Japanese War

The Chinese navy has arguably only engaged in one full-scale "modern" naval battle against a foreign opponent. By the early 1890s, China's navy was ranked eighth in the world, with a total of 65 ships, compared to Japan's eleventh ranking with only 32 ships. Immediately prior to the beginning of the Sino-Japanese War, one British admiral even claimed that China's Navy "would prove more than a match for the Japanese at sea; in fact, the Japanese would not be in it."[1] Within each separate fleet, however, there was a notable

---

1 Barry M. Blechman and Robert P. Berman, *Guide to Far Eastern Navies* (Annapolis, MD: Naval Institute Press, 1978), 76; Quoting an August 16, 1905 edition of *Japan Mail*.

lack of central authority. As described by William Tyler, the Beiyang fleet was like a "machine" whose "complexity lay in a vast muddle of diverse motives and ideals." Instead of order, from the Viceroy down to the director of the arsenal, the interlocking "wheels revolved to no general purpose but only to their own." In the midst of this confusion, there could be no "homogeneity of purpose," but only a "monstrously disordered epicyclic heterogeneity."[2] The lack of a unified naval structure, both to connect the various fleets and to direct them efficiently as individual units, proved to be an enormous disadvantage for the Chinese navy.

The September 17, 1894 Battle of the Yellow Sea set the course of the Sino-Japanese War. Admiral Ding Ruchang and the other high-ranking Chinese officers came from the Army and so were woefully untrained in modern naval strategy and tactics. On the day of the battle, Admiral Ding's ten ships were sailing in what has widely been described as a wedge-shaped formation.[3] According to Tyler, Commodore Liu Buchan made this change to save his own skin: "With the battleships in the center and the weakest vessels on the wings, the enemy would give the latter first attention; it would be a respite for a time, for an hour perhaps or more; it would avoid the immediate concentrating fire on his ship that would result from Line Ahead."[4]

This formation may have allowed the Chinese battleships to use maximum firepower but greatly reduced the maneuverability of the Chinese fleet when the Japanese divided their fleet into two squadrons. The main strategic goal of the Japanese fleet was to destroy the Chinese flagship. Within minutes a shell damaged the upper half of the central mast, which disrupted Admiral Ding's ability to signal his fleet with flags. Also, a lucky Japanese shot hit *Ding Yuan*'s

---

2 William Ferdinand Tyler, *Pulling Strings in China* (New York: Richard R. Smith, 1930), 41.
3 A description of this battle by Philo Norton McGiffin, clarified, "Our actual formation, which has justly been criticized, was an indent or zig zag line, [with] the two ironclads in the center." Lee McGiffin, *Yankee of the Yalu: Philo Norton McGiffin, American Captain in the Chinese Navy (1885–1895)* (New York: E. P. Dutton, 1968), 121.
4 Tyler, 49; Notably the *Zhongguo Haijun Baike Quanshu* (*Chinese Naval Encyclopedia*) does not comment on this incident, see 1271–72.

helm room, killing two men and destroying all of the signal flags. This action halted all further communication between the flagship and the Chinese fleet. Taking advantage of the Chinese ships' poor communications, the Japanese vessels dispersed and surrounded individual Chinese ships. Instead of remaining in formation, the Chinese ships also split up.

By failing to remain in formation and coordinate their fire, the Chinese fleet was sequentially decimated while the Japanese fleet weathered the battle without the loss of a single ship. In fact, during the four-and-a-half hours of battle, the Japanese rapid firing cannon poured thousands of shells into the Chinese ships; one Chinese battleship reportedly sustained over four hundred hits during the course of the battle. As a result, a total of four Chinese ships were sunk and there were over a thousand Chinese casualties.[5] By contrast to Japan's ample ordnance, inadequate supplies of ammunition was a huge problem for the Chinese ships: by 5:00 p.m. on the day of the battle, the 6-inch shells were gone and most of the 12-inch shells were also used up. On *Chen Yuan*, they only had three 12-inch shells left and these were loaded into the last three functioning guns. Fortunately for the Chinese, the Japanese may not have realized how little ammunition was left, and the battle ended by 5:45 p.m. This allowed the surviving Chinese ships to limp back to their main base at Port Arthur.

According to J. C. Perry, the major reason for Japan's success over China was that "the Japanese fleet was newer and far better equipped than the Chinese. The quick firing guns of the Japanese cruisers gave them immense advantage over their foe." But, another reason was also clear to him: the Japanese "men were far better trained and disciplined" than the Chinese.[6] In the end, it was Japan's effective use of their foreign-made ships and weapons that turned the tide of the battle. Regionalism was also an important factor. Perhaps paying the North back for the Sino-French War, when the Beiyang fleet had declined to come to the South's aid in 1884, China's three other regional fleets refused to come to Beiyang's assistance.

---

5 Rainer Falkenberg, *Constantin von Hanneken: Briefe aus China 1879–1886* (Koln, Germany: Bohlau Verlag GmbH, 1998), 349–59.
6 J. C. Perry "The Battle off the Tayang, 17 September 1894," *The Mariner's Mirror* 50, 3 (August 1964), 258.

Lesson: Japan defeated China in 1894 through better training and more effective use of foreign equipment. While China possessed superior German-made ships, and so theoretically should have won the conflict, it used these assets poorly. During the last days of the war, a remarkable lack of army–navy jointness was displayed when the Chinese army failed to spike the guns at Weihaiwei port in Shandong province. When the Japanese took the port, they could train the Chinese guns on the Beiyang ships trapped in the harbor. Chinese jointness among regional fleets was also institutionally and operationally difficult, which meant that Japan only opposed a fraction of the Chinese navy at any one time. The PLAN is currently divided into three separate fleets, which is similar to that in the 1890s. Likewise, the PLAN is often commanded by officers with little or no actual naval experience, official corruption can be a serious problem, and only since 2000 has the PLAN begun to discuss the need to increase joint training by advocating that various fleets should actively "conduct combined operations together."[7] Arguably, the PLAN has never really been in a full-scale naval battle. If the Chinese navy were to engage a foreign navy in battle today, it might face a fate similar to the Chinese Imperial Navy in 1894.

---

7 "Troops of China's Three Armed Services Are Being Assembled in Shantou," *Hong Kong Wen Wei Po*, 27 August 2001.

Chapter 9

CHINESE DECISION TO SINK THE NATIONALIST NAVY AS BLOCKSHIPS (1937)

Destruction of valuable naval equipment appeared during the second Sino-Japanese War (1937–45). While during its first war with Japan, Chinese naval officers sought to conserve their equipment, in the second war it was perhaps wasted needlessly. Specifically, during the second Sino-Japanese War the bulk of the Nationalist navy was sunk as blockships in what soon became clear was a useless effort to slow the Japanese advance up the Yangzi River. Competing Chinese fleets even matched each other to sink more ships. In the end, scuttling the Nationalist navy did not stop the Japanese. Since many of the sunken ships were in shallow waters, they could be salvaged and used by the Japanese invaders. For example, *Ninghai* and *Pinghai* were successfully refloated, adopted into the Japanese Imperial Navy, and renamed *Mikura* and *Mishima*.

Summary of the Nationalist Blockship Strategy

A blockship is a vessel deliberately sunk to prevent the use of a river, canal, or harbor. It may either be sunk by a navy defending the waterway to prevent the ingress of attacking enemy forces, or it may be brought by enemy raiders and used to prevent the waterway from being transited by the defending forces. This practice goes back many centuries. In China, it was a long-time tactic of the Chinese navy to block any maritime threat to China's internal rivers and canals by clogging harbors with log booms and chains strung from a row of floating junks. A famous battle scene in the 1966 Hollywood blockbuster *Sand Pebbles* takes place over destroying just such a river obstacle.

In 1930, Chiang Kai-shek appointed Admiral Ch'en Shao-kuan (1889–1969) the acting Minister of the Navy, and in 1932 he became the full Minister. Ch'en adopted an ambitious naval program, which envisioned 71 first-line ships, including battleships, cruisers, destroyers, submarines, and carriers, plus a total of 34 support ships, including submarines, depot ships, mine sweepers, torpedo boats, and hospital ships. The formation of this new force was to be divided into a Central, Northeast, and Guangdong Navy, with the Central navy being the largest and composed of two regular squadrons and a training squadron, the Northeast Navy accounting for the second fleet, and the Guangdong navy accounting for the third.

Although a handful of its ships were technically capable, the Chinese navy was poorly organized and led. According to Captain Baillie-Grohman, a British naval attaché sent to observe the Chinese navy, there is "no initiative anywhere, orders are always awaited." Even though the squadrons were organized to increase efficiency, it was "purely a paper one, and ships are moved round at a moment's notice without any reference to the Flag Officer under whom they are supposed to be." The biggest handicap was lack of a coherent policy. The equipment and armament were not standard, the ships were a "compromise between river and seagoing craft," and the lack of "<u>regular</u> funds" made the navy's existence precarious. The British naval attaché concluded: "It is in fact likely that the hand to mouth policy for the Chinese Admiralty will continue for some time yet."[1]

The most difficult problem was poor leadership. Many Chinese naval officers had little or no modern training. For those who did, it was not uncommon for them to be overlooked for promotion and forced to leave the service. For example, two out of three American-trained officers left the navy soon after their return to China, one Japanese-trained student quickly committed suicide in despair, and even the British-trained officers were all given shore appointments against the advice of the British naval attaché, who strongly

---

[1] "Naval Mission in China, 1931–1932, Report by Captain Baillie-Grohman, with index," British National Archives, Adm 1/8756/133, 55; underlining in original.

recommended to Admiral Ch'en that "these Officers ought to have sea appointments."² When challenged as to why these better-trained officers were not put in charge of ocean-going ships, Admiral Ch'en explained that such rapid promotion would make the older, less trained, officers lose "face."³ This cultural attitude almost guaranteed that the Chinese navy was not utilizing its best officers to their fullest.

Throughout the early 1930s, the Central and the Northeast fleets of the Chinese navy drew closer together, but did not become truly united. This meant that China lost a golden opportunity to prepare its navy for the next great challenge, this time from Japan. When disaster struck in 1937, the Chinese navy would be ill prepared to face this new threat. In response to the Japanese army invasion of central China, the Nationalist navy was arranged so as to blockade the Yangzi River and defend the Jiangyin forts from attack. During August 1937, the *Pinghai*, *Ninghai*, *Yingrui*, and *Yatsen* held off the Japanese for almost fifty days. On September 23, 1937, however, Japanese bombers sank the *Pinghai* and the *Ninghai* in shallow water, which allowed them to be refloated later and added to the Japanese navy. After bitter fighting, the Chinese naval defenses were broken by early December 1937.

The Chinese made liberal use of blockships. On August 12, 1937, the Nationalists deliberately scuttled "eight older warships, twenty merchant ships, and eight barges [...] to serve as blockships." This plan failed to halt the Japanese advance, however, and over the next month the Japanese sank China's best warships. On September 25, another four cruisers, *Hai Chi*, *Hai Rong*, *Hai Chou*, and *Hai Chen*, were also scuttled: "It had not been intended to sacrifice all four cruisers; however, incredibly, two of these had become blockships *unwillingly*. Considering the fierce fight he had put up personally and losing his best ships, First Fleet commander Chen Shaokuan demand[ed] that the other two cruisers not belonging to the Min [Fleet] be scuttled as well! This is reluctantly agreed upon and carried out."⁴

Following Japan's 1937 invasion of China, the Nationalist navy proved to be inadequate to counter the Japanese Imperial Navy, so the vast bulk of the Chinese naval ships were eventually sunk in

---

2 Ibid., 76.
3 Ibid., 77.
4 http://www.combinedfleet.com/Destruction.htm; italics in the original.

the Yangzi River. This proved to be a futile effort to block Japan's invasion upriver. By 1939, the *China Year Book* reported that "except for a few warships which have been salvaged by the Japanese, the Chinese navy would appear to have been completely destroyed."[5] In 1940, Chiang Kai-shek ordered that the Navy Ministry be dissolved.[6] Thus, a Chinese naval force that had taken over a decade to build was quickly disbanded and destroyed to ensure it would not fall into enemy hands.

Lesson: Waste of valuable naval ships led to the disbanding of the Nationalist navy. According to one estimate, China had over 120 ships totaling more than 68,000 tons in 1937, but scuttled and sank over a hundred ships—many of them of modern construction—in a hopeless attempt to impede easy access for Japanese forces.[7] Jealousies between fleet commanders perhaps resulted in more ships being scuttled than was absolutely necessary, since Ch'en Shao-kuan insisted that a naval rival and counterpart match his two-ship sacrifice. Many ships were also scuttled in shallow water, which meant that they could be easily salvaged by the Japanese. In the end, the Nationalist blockships had no lasting impact on slowing the Japanese invasion into Central China. On the contrary, Japan's eventual acquisition of Nationalist ships may have assisted its offensive campaigns against the United States.

---

5 *The China Year Book 1939* (Shanghai, China: The North-China Daily News & Herald, 1939), 598.
6 Swanson, *Eighth Voyage of the Dragon*, 166.
7 Yu Zufan, *The Real Record of the Chinese Fleet (Zhongguo Jiandui Shi Lu)*, (Chunfeng Literature and Arts Publishing House, 1997), 15–16.

Chapter 10

CHONGQING MUTINY ALLOWING THE PLA TO CROSS THE YANGZI RIVER (1949)

On February 25, 1949, the Nationalist flagship *Chongqing* mutinied. Prior to this event, it was widely assumed by many foreign commentators that China would be cut in half at the Yangzi River, just as Germany and Korea had been divided. Joseph Stalin hoped a divided China, with both parts of roughly equal size, would cancel each other out and leave China weak and easily influenced by the USSR. Once the rest of the Nationalist navy guarding the river also mutinied, however, this allowed the Communists to cross the Yangzi River into southern China. When the Nationalists fled to Taiwan, the Communists easily dominated all of Mainland China. After the PRC was created in 1949, within 10 years the larger-than-expected PRC was to turn from a Soviet ally to one of the USSR's greatest enemies.

Summary of the *Chongqing* Mutiny

The most famous twentieth-century Chinese mutiny was the case of the Nationalist flagship *Chongqing*, formerly the *H.M.S. Aurora*. The British government gave the 5,270-ton *Aurora* to China in May 1948. Far larger and more modern than China's other ships, *Aurora* was equipped with 6 six-inch guns, 6 twenty-one inch torpedo tubes, and manned by a crew of 450. Upon arrival in China, *Aurora* was renamed *Chongqing* in honor of the Nationalist's wartime capital. When *Chongqing* mutinied on February 25, 1949, it undermined Chiang Kai-shek's Mandate of Heaven. The rest of the Nationalist fleet soon followed. This gave the Chinese Communist forces an unforeseen and largely unhindered opportunity to cross the Yangzi River and consolidate power throughout southern China.

During 1948, *Chongqing* became the flagship of the Chinese navy and was assigned the task of standing guard against a possible Chinese Communist invasion across the Yangzi River into southern China. Although the Chinese government had spent an estimated ten million pounds to train the crew and deliver *Chongqing* to China, the poor treatment of the crew and arrears in pay led to numerous desertions. It was also reported that the popular captain of the ship was to be replaced in late February. Morale was low, even before *Chongqing* was assigned to the dangerous task of guarding the Yangzi River.

On February 25, 1949, *Chongqing* mutinied and deserted from the Nationalists to the Communists, fleeing north toward Manchuria. *Chongqing's* first port of call was the coastal city of Qifu, in Shandong province, which was the former summer operating base of the US Asiatic Fleet. Qifu was at that time in Communist hands, however, and as reported by Walter Sullivan, "it is believed that Communist China now has the only major warship under the Red banner outside those of the Russian Navy."[1] Nationalist bombers tried, and failed, to sink *Chongqing* while it was in Qifu.

Chasing the fleeing ship northward, Nationalist ships followed as *Chongqing* anchored close to the northern shore of the Bohai Gulf, on its way to Dalian. On March 11, 1949, Nationalist sources reported that they had sunk *Chongqing*. But as later reports showed, these early claims were exaggerated, and eyewitnesses stated that when the *Chongqing* docked at Dalian, she "appeared to be undamaged."[2] Finally, in March 18 and 19, 1949, two Nationalist air force raids located *Chongqing* at rest near the South Manchurian port of Huludao. *Chongqing* was attacked by Nationalist airplanes and it was reported at the time that "a Chinese Air Force photograph […] had shown the former *H.M.S. Aurora*, a gift from Britain to China, lying on her side with a gaping hole in her stern."[3] Although *Chongqing* did not sink immediately, she was sufficiently damaged that the Communist

---

1 Walter Sullivan, "Nanking's Cruiser Deserts to Enemy," *New York Times*, March 2, 1949.
2 "Chinese Cruiser in Dairen," *New York Times*, March 14, 1949.
3 "Cruiser Loss Confirmed," *New York Times*, March 26, 1949.

leaders decided to scuttle her after stripping the ship of her most valuable equipment.

The *Chongqing* mutiny had an enormous impact on the ongoing Nationalist–Communist civil war. When news of the mutiny first appeared, the symbolism of the Nationalist flagship defecting helped bolster the Communists' standing and gave the Communist leaders enormous face. Chinese Communist Party Chairman Mao Zedong and Commander-in-chief of the PLA Zhu De quickly sent a cable congratulating the *Chongqing's* crew, announcing, "the Chinese people must build a powerful national defence and, besides the ground forces, must have their own air force and navy."[4]

Conversely, the loss of their navy's flagship was a major embarrassment to the Nationalist leaders. Named for the Nationalists' revolutionary capital, Chongqing, the defection of this ship threatened to be an insurmountable loss of face for the Nationalist cause. It was also widely interpreted by the Chinese people as a sign that the Nationalists had lost the Mandate of Heaven. On April 20, 1949, most of the rest of the Yangzi fleet, under Commander Lin Zun, defected to the Communists. Among this fleet were included "one destroyer, three destroyer escorts, one patrol gunboat, five landing ships, and eight smaller auxiliaries."[5] According to PLAN sources, Lin brought a total of 30 ships and 1,271 sailors to the Communist side.[6] The PRC, therefore, dates the creation of the PLAN to April 23, 1949.

Chongqing had been given the all-important assignment of guarding the Yangzi River and making sure that the PLA troops could not cross into South China. Following these mutinies, however, the Yangzi crossings were left virtually undefended and vulnerable. As one source stated, "the Communists had no navy. Crossing the river heavily defended on its southern banks could be difficult. Stalin advised Mao and his associates not to cross the Yangzi. […] [But] In the summer

---

4 Lexis-Nexis, quoting the Xinhua News Agency from Wednesday, March 8, 1979.
5 Bruce Swanson, *Eighth Voyage of the Dragon: A History of China's Quest for Seapower* (Annapolis, MD: Naval Institute Press, 1982), 182.
6 *Zhongguo Haijun Baike Quanshu* (*Chinese Naval Encyclopedia*), 1269; According to Muller, however, Lin brought over only 25 ships and 1,200 sailors. David G. Muller, *China as a Maritime Power* (Boulder, CO: Westview Press, 1984), 11.

of 1949, the Communist forces swept across the river."[7] Without any means to halt the Communists' advance, the Nationalists were forced to retreat further south, and eventually evacuated to the offshore island of Taiwan. Unquestionably, the *Chongqing* mutiny played an extremely pivotal role in the Communists' military victory and the subsequent founding of the People's Republic of China on October 1, 1949.

Lesson: The *Chongqing* mutiny had an enormous and immediate impact on the Nationalists, forcing Chiang Kai-shek to lose face and undermining his government's Mandate of Heaven. The mutiny of the flagship undoubtedly spurred the defection of much of the rest of the Nationalist navy. Without a naval force to stop them from crossing the Yangzi River, the Chinese Communists invaded the south and quickly assumed control over all of Mainland China. After the creation of the PRC in 1949, Communist fears of a repetition of the *Chongqing* mutiny may have resulted in the revival of the multi-fleet structure of the nineteenth-century Qing navy. Rather than creating a unified navy, the PLAN's division into three separate regional fleets gave the Chinese Communists tremendous internal control; if one fleet were to mutiny, for example, then there would be two others loyal to the central government to put it down. However, this three-fleet structure contained many of the same nineteenth-century flaws as well, particularly in terms of poor communications, inadequate intra-fleet cooperation, and the PLAN's inability to conduct joint actions. Counterintuitively, as the PLAN modernizes and the regional fleets become increasingly joint, the possibility actually increases that a mutiny that breaks out in one part of the navy might spread to include much or perhaps even all of the Chinese navy.

---

7 http://www.fsmitha.com/h2/ch24cld8.htm

Chapter 11

THE TAIWAN STRAIT CRISES (1954–55 AND 1958)

Mao Zedong responded to a 1952–53 increase in Nationalist forces along the Taiwan Strait by signing an armistice in Korea, and then moving additional troops south. The first crisis in 1954–55 led to the evacuation of the Dachen Islands, off Zhejiang province, which was Chiang Kai-shek's home province, so this was considered a personal "loss of face" for him. In 1958, the Nationalists—with help from the US Navy—resisted PLA attempts to retake Jinmen Island, blocking Xiamen harbor. In both crises, politics trumped military strategy. Mao hoped to halt the Nationalist blockade, backed up by a US strategic embargo, which was undermining China's economy. Desperate to catch up, Mao's Great Leap Forward, 1958–1961, led to one of the worst famines in history, with an estimated 45 million Chinese perishing. Meanwhile, increasing tensions with the USSR eventually resulted in a split.

Summary of the Taiwan Strait Crises

During the Nationalist retreat from the mainland in 1949, the Republic of China (ROC) on Taiwan instituted a naval blockade of the People's Republic of China (PRC). Although the Nationalist navy was comparatively large, its forces were retained mainly for defense of Taiwan's coastal perimeter. To conduct the blockade, the Nationalists worked with a number of guerrilla movements located on offshore islands not far from China's coast. Later, the US Navy helped defend Taiwan even while providing military assistance—especially aircraft—that made air patrols of the blockade possible. The Nationalist blockade of the PRC lasted from 1949 through 1958.

A Communist attack on the Nationalist-held base on Jinmen Island (Quemoy) failed during October 1949. But Communist forces, in spite of naval and air inferiority, succeeded in overwhelming the Nationalist base on Hainan Island during February–April in 1950, the Zhoushan Archipelago during May 1950, and Tatan Island as late as July 1950. By the summer of 1950, therefore, the Nationalists had lost their crucial island bases in the Bo Hai, off the mouth of the Yangzi River, and on Hainan Island. Although the Communist victories diminished the blockade area by half, the Nationalists used their remaining offshore bases to continue their blockade of the ports of Shantou, Xiamen, Fuzhou, and Wenzhou, which were critical to deter the Communists from launching an invasion of Taiwan.

There was ample evidence that the Communist forces were preparing to mount an amphibious invasion of Taiwan, as the PLA began concentrating thousands of motorized junks in the port cities along the Taiwan Strait in preparation for a massive invasion.[1] According to one US Navy estimate, the Communists could assemble "7,000 merchant steamers and other large vessels" to transport 200,000 troops across the Strait.[2] But any possibility of a PRC attack was effectively countered at the beginning of the Korean War. On June 27, 1950, President Truman ordered the Seventh Fleet to move into the Taiwan Strait. The Chinese Communists condemned the neutralization policy as an aggressive action and demanded the fleet's withdrawal. The planned Chinese invasion of Taiwan was postponed to 1951, however, then to 1952, and eventually cancelled altogether.[3]

With any threat of a PRC invasion of Taiwan effectively countered by the US Navy, the Nationalist navy could adopt a more offensive policy, including using the offshore islands to mount attacks against the mainland and Communist-held islands, and against Communist-led "junk convoys" escorted by junks armed with small artillery pieces, mortars, and automatic weapons. Whenever possible, Nationalist

---

1 He Di, "The Last Campaign to Unify China," in Mark A. Ryan, David M. Finkelstein, and Michael A. McDevitt, eds., *Chinese Warfighting: The PLA Experience Since 1949* (Armonk, NY: M. E. Sharpe, 2003), 73–90.
2 Edward Marolda, "The U.S. Navy and the Chinese Civil War, 1945–1952," Ph.D. Dissertation, George Washington University, 1990, 159.
3 He Di, "The Last Campaign to Unify China," 84, 87–88.

ships would attack, surround, and sink the convoys. The Nationalists also used various offshore islands as listening posts to collect valuable intelligence on Mainland China. After May 1950, the only remaining full-time Nationalist blockade bases were on Jinmen and Mazu Islands.

After China intervened in the Korean War during the fall of 1950, the United States actively helped the Nationalists tighten their blockade. With American training, equipment, and financial backing, it was hoped that "the blockade of war goods, partially effective now, will grow more effective as the naval and air forces of Nationalist China are built up with U.S. aid."[4] Due to a rapid decline in the relative capacity of the Nationalist navy, however, by early 1954, immediately before tensions erupted over control of Jinmen and Mazu, the Nationalist held only 25 islands, down from 32 the year before.[5]

During 1954–55, and again in 1958, China tried to break the blockade. Stopping Nationalist attacks by sea and air became one of the PRC's highest objectives. In 1954, there were 32 incidents in which Nationalist forces attacked British shipping. During this period, "Warship incidents have been steadily decreasing and in recent times aircraft incidents have been predominant."[6] In November 1954, PRC leaders explained to the visiting Indian prime minister, Jawaharlal Nehru, that the Nationalists from their offshore bases were conducting "nuisance raids and interference with shipping." Nehru warned the British high commissioner in India that China was "determined not to tolerate this situation any longer."[7] With the outbreak of the first ROC–PRC crisis later that month, the PLA eventually retook the Dachen Islands, the northernmost offshore islands used in the blockade, located in Chiang Kai-shek's home province; with US army and naval backing, however, the Nationalists had fully evacuated the Dachen Islands in early February 1955.

---

4 "China Blockade: How It Works; Ships by the U.S.—Sailors by Chiang Kai-shek," *U.S. News and World Report*, February 20, 1953.
5 "The Struggle for the Coastal Islands of China," *The ONI Review Supplement*, December 1953, I–IX.
6 "China: Interference with British Merchant Shipping (Secret)," 1955, British National Archives (hereafter BNA), ADM 116/6245.
7 UK High Commissioner in India Report of Meeting with Prime Minister Nehru (Secret), November 10, 1954, BNA, FO 371/110238.

During December 1954, Taiwan and the United States signed a bilateral mutual-security pact reaffirming that the United States would defend Taiwan and the Penghus. However, it was less clear about protecting offshore islands: "The pact will be deliberately vague about how the U.S. might react if the Reds were to invade any of the other Nationalist-held islands off the China coast. The U.S. doesn't want the Reds to know which it will defend, and which it will simply write off. It prefers to keep them guessing."[8] A secret agreement signed by Chiang Kai-shek and Secretary of State Dulles stated that Chiang would not initiate offensive action against the mainland without first seeking the approval of the United States.[9]

In January 1955, Congress passed the "Formosa Resolution" stating that the US president would judge whether a PRC attack on the offshore islands was part of an invasion of Taiwan.[10] Washington, fearful that the developing crisis in the Taiwan strait could lead to a general war, asked Taipei to consider giving up its bases on Jinmen and Mazu. In return, President Eisenhower promised to create a joint US–Taiwan "defense zone" from Shantou to Wenzhou "in which the movement of all seaborne traffic of a contraband or war-making character would be interdicted." In particular, the US Navy would be responsible for setting mine fields that "would force coastwise junk traffic to come out where it also could be intercepted and controlled." Chiang Kai-shek refused, arguing that once he gave up Jinmen and Mazu, the United States would quickly halt any "effective shipping interdiction scheme in the face of strong and inevitable opposition by the British and others."[11]

With the Taiwanese–PRC naval balance shifting in favor of the PLAN, the Nationalists held the remaining offshore islands only by default. The Communist army and naval forces were considered capable of taking the offshore islands with massive force, of by-passing the offshore islands entirely and striking for Taiwan, or continuing

---

8 "Pressure and a Pact," *Newsweek*, December 13, 1954.
9 Bruce A. Elleman, *Taiwan's Offshore Islands: Pathway or Barrier?* (Newport, RI: NWC Press, 2019), 47–48.
10 Harold C. Hinton, *China's Turbulent Quest* (New York: Macmillan, 1972), 68.
11 "Memorandum for the Record, by the Ambassador in the Republic of China (Rankin)," April 29, 1955, China; 1955–57, Vol. II, *FRUS*, 529–31.

their "hit-and-run campaign against individual islands, without apparent plan." By the mid-1950s, the new air phase of the blockade was beginning to lose steam, the number of attacks declined, while the overall impact of the blockade was described by one source as strategically "puny."[12] However, as late as June 1957, the Nationalist government was still warning foreign shipping entering Communist ports that they did so at "their own risk."[13]

When the second cross-strait crisis broke out in August 1958, Prince Norodom Sihanouk, the president of the Council of Ministers of Cambodia, visited China to mediate with Mao Zedong and Zhou Enlai. In mid-September, Prince Sihanouk explained to Walter S. Robertson, assistant secretary to the US Mission to the UN, that the PRC leaders were "concerned by the fact that the offshore islands are being used to mount Commando attacks on the mainland and to impose a blockade." US negotiators argued back that "shipping has been moving freely out of Chinese ports for the last two years," and they denied that the islands were "used for aggressive purposes."[14]

Washington's support for the Nationalists' continued hold over the offshore islands was not a blank check. On August 23, 1958, the PRC began to shell Jinmen. In October 1958, Secretary-of-State John Foster Dulles tried to persuade Taiwan to reduce the number of Nationalist forces on the islands, even while halting "commando raids and blockades."[15] Attempting to ease tensions, Dulles even flew to Taiwan and convinced Chiang Kai-shek "to renounce the use of force in an attempt to reunify China."[16] In return for Chiang agreeing to reduce forces on Jinmen by "not less than 15,000 men" Dulles agreed to greater arms shipments, including "a minimum of 12 240 mm howitzers," a "minimum of 12 155 mm guns," the possibility of "Lacrosse missiles to be considered at a later date," a

---

12 "The Struggle for the Coastal Islands of China," *The ONI Review Supplement*, December 1953, I–IX.
13 *The New York Times*, June 6, 1957.
14 "Memorandum of Conversation," September 16, 1958, China; 1958–1960, Vol. XIX, *FRUS*, 201–203.
15 Foreign Office to Washington (Secret), October 22, 1958, BNA, PREM 11/3738.
16 Letter from John Foster Dulles to British Ambassador (Secret), October 25, 1958, BNA, FO 371/133543.

"minimum of 1 tank battalion" plus if changes to the M-8 assault gun "proves feasible, provide sufficient converted vehicles to motorized [sic] 2 battalions of infantry."[17] This secret agreement effectively ended the Nationalist's decade-long naval blockade of China, which had already lasted longer than any other modern naval blockade up until this time.[18]

Lesson: Naval blockades and strategic embargoes can produce dramatic effects. The Nationalist blockade succeeded in interdicting China's coastal and international trade. The PRC had to make up the losses by redirecting its trade over land via the Soviet Union, which helped exacerbate Sino-Soviet tensions; before World War II, only 1 percent of China's foreign trade was with the USSR, while by 1957, this figure had increased to 50 percent.[19] Overreliance on Moscow restricted Beijing's diplomatic leverage, so that it could not negotiate equitable relations. Increasing tensions soon led to the Sino-Soviet "split." The blockade also had profound geopolitical consequences on a large number of islands right off China's southeastern coastline, including the evacuation of the Dachens and the militarization of both Jinmen and Mazu. Since 1958, the offshore islands have acted as one of the most reliable barometers of China–Taiwan relations. Should the PRC ever attempt to "blockade" or invade Taiwan, reducing the offshore islands would almost certainly be part of any successful military strategy.[20]

---

17 Memorandum for Major John S. Eisenhower, December 11, 1958, Dwight D. Eisenhower Papers, White House Office, Staff, International Series, Boc 3, File "China (1) Sept. 1958-April 1960."
18 Elleman, *Taiwan's Offshore Islands*, 47–48.
19 "Notes on Sino-Soviet Relations," 1958, FO 371/133366.
20 Piers M. Wood and Charles D. Ferguson, "How China Might Invade Taiwan," *Naval War College Review* 54, 4 (Autumn 2001).

Chapter 12

CHINA'S DECISION TO TAKE THE PARACEL ISLANDS FROM SOUTH VIETNAM (1974)

Foreign navies can choose whether to intervene or stay out of Asian conflicts. With North Vietnam poised to retake the South, and following closely upon President Richard Nixon's visit to China in 1972, the US Navy stood aside as Chinese naval forces took the Paracel Islands by force from Vietnam in 1974. What made this decision somewhat unusual is the islands were claimed by South Vietnam, which was a US ally at the time. It is likely that the US government preferred the PRC—at that point a US ally against the USSR—to obtain these strategic islands rather than let them fall to North Vietnam—at that point a Soviet ally. Thus, the decision was made in Washington not to interfere with the PLAN's first major expeditionary attack by sea against a foreign country since the formation of the PRC in 1949.

Summary of China's 1974 Naval Expedition

China's 1974 naval expedition to claim the Paracel Islands was arguably the first time that the PLAN conducted naval expeditionary operations against a foreign enemy.[1] The Chinese name for this naval expedition is *Xisha Ziwei Fanjizhan* (西沙自衛反擊戰), or

---

1 There were a number of PRC naval expeditions against Hainan and the offshore islands during the 1950s, but most of these were close to shore and were considered to be part of China's "domestic" conflict with the Nationalist government on Taiwan.

"Counterattack in Self-Defense in the Paracel Islands."[2] China argues that it was a necessary response to oppose Vietnamese attempts to force Chinese fishermen out of the Paracel Islands, a traditional Chinese fishing ground. Others have challenged this view, however, focusing instead on China's efforts to oppose Vietnam's reunification, as reflected in increased border incidents intended to shift Hanoi's "military attention away from South Vietnam."[3]

The 1974 Sino-Vietnamese conflict over the Paracel Islands must also be put into the context of the problems undermining Sino-Soviet relations. Following their formal "split" in 1960, Sino-Soviet relations through the late 1960s were marred not only by sharp disagreement over the status of Outer Mongolia, but also by numerous territorial disputes along their mutual border. The 1969 border clashes gave the PLA confidence that it could counter the Red Army, opening an opportunity during 1971 for China to adopt a new foreign policy initiative by promoting friendly relations with the United States. This culminated in President Richard Nixon's historic trip during February 21–28, 1972, to Beijing and the signing of the *Shanghai Communiqué*.

After Nixon's much-publicized visit to China, Mao Zedong endorsed a major military modernization program that called for developing an ocean-going navy, as well as the continued expansion of coastal defense. This gave the PLAN the tools that it would need if China sought to move southward into the South China Sea. Perhaps concerned that a unified Vietnam might fall further under Soviet influence, the PRC decided to take possession of the Paracel Islands from South Vietnam immediately prior to the North Vietnamese reunification of the country.

On January 19, 1974, the PLA Navy seized the Paracel Islands. According to the Chinese version of these events, the conflict originated when the South Vietnamese illegally arrested Chinese fishermen during November 1973, prompting the Chinese foreign ministry to announce on January 11, 1974, that Vietnam had invaded its sovereign territory. The main conflict occurred in the morning of January 19, when four Vietnamese vessels encountered an equal

---

2 杨志本 (Yang Zhiben, ed.), 中国海军百科全书 (China Navy Encyclopedia), vol. 2 (Beijing: 海潮出版社 (Sea Tide Press), 1998), 1747.
3 Hemen Ray, *China's Vietnam War* (New Delhi: Radiant Publishers, 1983), 58.

number of Chinese ships. The battle lasted less than an hour, but resulted in the sinking of one Vietnamese ship, and damage to the other three. While the Chinese ships also sustained damage, none of them sank.[4]

Deng Xiaoping was chief of the PLA general staff at the time and oversaw the operation.[5] Considering the distances involved and the time it took to deploy the PLAN ships to the area, the date of the January 19 battle—on exactly the 24th anniversary of the PRC's recognition of the North Vietnamese government—was clearly not a coincidence.[6] It sent a political signal to North Vietnam, showing Beijing's displeasure with Hanoi's close relations with Moscow. On January 20, these islands were officially annexed by the PRC and made an integral part of Guangdong province.

By the end of January 1974, the PLAN had consolidated control over the Paracel Islands. Following the formal reunification of Vietnam in 1975, the Communist government in Hanoi openly split with Beijing. On July 1, 1976, Vietnam stated that the Paracel Islands were Vietnamese territory. In response, "China recalled several groups of specialists from Vietnam and delayed work on a number of projects being built with Chinese aid."[7] Ever since, Sino-Vietnamese tensions over the islands have persisted. As one Vietnamese scholar has clarified, the Paracel Islands are "strategically important" to Vietnam, since they are "located on one of the world's most important sea-lanes."[8]

The PRC's decision to take the Paracel Islands contributed to tensions that resulted in armed conflict. The Sino-Vietnamese war of 1979, fought mainly over land boundaries, also included sharp

---

4 杨志本 (Yang Zhiben, ed.), 中国海军百科全书 (China Navy Encyclopedia), vol. 2 (Beijing: 海潮出版社 (Sea Tide Press), 1998), 1747.
5 David G. Muller, *China as a Maritime Power* (Boulder, CO: Westview Press, 1984), 86–90.
6 For more on this issue, see Bruce A. Elleman, "Sino-Soviet Relations and the February 1979 Sino-Vietnamese Conflict," (April 20, 1996), at http://www.mtholyoke.edu/acad/intrel/vietnam.htm.
7 Stephen J. Morris, *Why Vietnam Invaded Cambodia: Political Culture and the Causes of War* (Stanford, CA: Stanford University Press, 1999), 174.
8 Nguyen Van Canh, *Vietnam under Communism, 1975–1982* (Stanford, CA: Hoover Institution Press, 1983), 242.

divisions over maritime claims in the South China Sea.[9] On February 15, 1979, Deng declared that China planned to conduct a limited attack on Vietnam. To prevent Soviet intervention, China put its troops along the Sino-Soviet border—estimated at one-and-a-half million—on an emergency war alert, set up a new military command in Xinjiang, and even evacuated an estimated 300,000 civilians from their homes immediately along the Sino-Soviet border.[10]

Meanwhile, the PLAN's South Sea Fleet deployed 2 missile destroyers, 4 missile escort destroyers, 27 patrol boats, 20 submarines, and 604 other vessels. In addition to stationing patrol boats around the Paracel Islands, the 1,000-man garrison manned anti-aircraft guns. The Paracel Islands served both as a buffer area between the PRC and Vietnam, and also potentially as a strategic "area to stage punitive naval strikes against the Vietnamese."[11] Chinese land and naval forces in the Paracel Islands further provided an important forward "outpost" to observe the Soviet Navy.

On March 5, 1979, China announced a troop withdrawal from Vietnam—timed to correspond exactly with the 26th anniversary of Stalin's death—and on April 3, Beijing informed Moscow that it had no intention of renewing its 1950 Sino-Soviet friendship treaty. Meanwhile, Vietnam, chastened by its poor showing in 1979, now "stations 700,000 combat troops in the northern portion of the country."[12] When peace talks opened during April 1979, China immediately demanded that Vietnam recognize PRC sovereignty in the South China Sea, and in particular over the Paracel Islands, but Hanoi rejected this proposal.

Tensions remained high, and in 1988, a second conflict broke out in the Spratly Islands, as Chinese naval forces drove Vietnamese

---

9 Pao-Min Chang, *The Sino-Vietnamese Territorial Dispute* (New York: Praeger, 1986), 86.
10 Robert A. Scalapino, "Asia in a Global Context: Strategic Issue for the Soviet Union," in Richard H. Solomon and Masataka Kosaka, eds., *The Soviet Far East Military Buildup* (Dover, MA., Auburn House, 1986), 28.
11 Steven J. Hood, *Dragons Entangled: Indochina and the China-Vietnam War* (Armonk, NY: M. E. Sharpe, 1992), 129.
12 Karl D. Jackson, "Indochina, 1982–1985: Peace Yields to War," in Richard H. Solomon and Masataka Kosaka, eds., *The Soviet Far East Military Buildup* (Dover, MA., Auburn House, 1986), 206.

troops from Johnson Reef. On April 13, 1988, China incorporated the Paracels and the Spratlys into its newly established Hainan Province.[13] Most recently, on December 4, 2007, China announced it had just created a new "city" in Hainan Province in November to administer the Paracels, Macclesfield Bank, and the Spratlys, even though China's sovereignty over these islands remains in dispute. According to one recent assessment of Sino-Vietnamese relations, the "Paracels remain a standing bilateral issue that is unlikely to be resolved."[14]

Lesson: Intervention in a foreign conflict is highly visible, while the decision not to intervene is often overlooked or ignored. To a large degree, therefore, decisions not to intervene during a crisis can be described as the "negative space" of history. Yet, as shown by this example, a US government decision not to intervene in a regional conflict can clearly produce a rapid and long-term change in the balance of power. In 1974, Washington ordered the US Navy to stand aside and let China take the Paracel Islands from a US ally, South Vietnam. Perhaps Washington preferred that China control these strategic islands, rather than let either North Vietnam or, worse yet, Hanoi's Soviet ally take control of them. Forty years later, however, PRC control of these strategic islands has given it a base of operations to claim even greater territory in the South China Sea, a policy that the United States opposes.

---

13 Sheldon W. Simon, "ASEAN Security in the 1990s," *Asian Survey* 29, 6 (1989), 595.
14 Brantly Womack, *China and Vietnam: The Politics of Asymmetry* (New York: Cambridge University Press, 2006), 253.

Chapter 13

MISSILE BLOCKADE: THE TAIWAN STRAIT CRISIS (1995–96)

A naval show of force can have a dramatic impact. Almost 50 years to the day after the Potsdam Conference of July 16–August 2, 1945, resulting in the Potsdam Declaration of July 26, 1945, which reconfirmed the Cairo Declaration signed two years before stating that Taiwan should be returned to China, the PRC conducted six missile tests during July 21–26, 1995, in an area only 40 nautical miles north of Taiwan's Pengchiayu Island. These tests interfered with both sea and air traffic to-and-from Taiwan, and ignited international outrage. In March 1996, a second series of missile tests sought to influence Taiwan's presidential election. The second attempt also failed, however, and Lee Teng-hui became the first democratically elected president in all of Chinese history. China's actions have since been described as a "missile blockade."[1] They led to the intervention of two US Navy carrier battle groups in support of Taiwan.

Summary of the Taiwan "Missile Blockade" Crisis

The July 1995 missile tests by the PRC are often portrayed as a response to the granting of an American visa to Taiwan's president Lee Teng-hui for an unofficial visit to Cornell University in early June 1995. However, the real underlying concern for the PRC was over Taiwan's rapid democratization and the growing separatist claims by large numbers of Taiwanese. On July 18, 1995, China announced

---

1 Chris Rahman, "Ballistic Missiles in China's Anti-Taiwan Blockade Strategy," in Bruce Elleman and S. C. M. Paine, eds., *Naval Blockades and Seapower: Strategies and Counter-Strategies, 1805–2005* (London: Routledge, 2006), 215–23.

that ballistic missile tests would take place between 21 and 28 of July. These dates exactly corresponded with the fiftieth anniversary of the 1945 Potsdam treaty stating that China would regain all territories lost to Japan, including Taiwan, after World War II ended.

The PRC missile tests were intended to create an exclusion zone, in this case a ten-nautical-mile circle, in which ships and planes could not enter safely. This zone was located about 85 miles north of Taiwan, which was just outside Taiwan's sovereign waters but actively interfered with flight paths and shipping lanes. Six DF-15 (CSS-6/M-9) short-range ballistic missiles (SRBMs) were fired, two each on July 21, 22, and 23, 1995. Beijing's announcement warned other states "against entering the said sea area and air space" during the firing period. These PRC missile tests diverted hundreds of commercial flights heading for Taipei.[2] From 15 to 25 in August 1995, PRC military exercises, including about 20 warships and 40 aircraft, were held in a large area to the northwest of the SRBM splash zone. During this period, the PRC tested both anti-ship missiles and anti-aircraft missiles.

In response to these heightened tensions the US Navy sailed the USS *Nimitz* (CVN 68) through the Taiwan Strait on December 19, 1995 on its way to the Indian Ocean. The stated reason for transiting the strait, rather than going east of Taiwan, was poor weather. The PRC did not seem to know about, or simply did not acknowledge, the transit. But on January 27, 1996, the *United Daily News* and *New York Times* reported it. This was the first time an American aircraft carrier had transited the Taiwan Strait since the late 1970s. Whether intentional or not, it sent a sharp signal to Beijing not to interfere in Taiwan's domestic politics.

In response to this perceived US show of force, Beijing warned the Assistant Secretary of Defense, Chas Freeman, that the PRC would launch one missile per day against Taiwan for a period of 30 days if Taipei continued on its path toward formal independence. A Chinese official apparently threatened Washington with nuclear retaliation,

---

2 Richard D. Fisher, "China's Missiles over the Taiwan Strait: A Political and Military Assessment," in James R. Lilley and Chuck Downs, eds., *Crisis in the Taiwan Strait* (Washington, DC: American Enterprise Institute for Public Policy Research, 1997), 170–71.

even warning Freeman that the US Navy should not intervene in a cross-Strait crisis, because US leaders "care more about Los Angeles than they do about Taiwan."[3] China's one-missile-per-day strategy and its implied threat against the United States were both reminiscent of similar PRC pressure tactics during the 1950s against Jinmen and Mazu Islands.

The PRC tests during March 18–25, 1996, were timed to put pressure on Taiwan's presidential election, scheduled for March 23. CinCPac Admiral Joseph Prueher's immediate reaction was to "send a carrier." His plan was to "put *Independence* east of Taiwan, and put two Aegis cruisers north and south. [...] Got them there fast. Got them there quietly."[4] Soon, US aircraft were patrolling about 100 miles off of Taiwan. The USS *Nimitz* carrier group was also ordered to return from the Persian Gulf at high speed. Other naval assets included two Aegis guided-missile cruisers and US Air Force RC-135 Rivet Joint electronic surveillance aircraft.[5] As a result of sending *Independence*, and later supporting her with *Nimitz*, the Chinese only fired five missiles, three north and two south of Taiwan, instead of the larger number that they had planned.[6] When Chinese diplomats later told him "you punched us in the nose," Prueher's reaction was, "Not so, we reacted in a measured way. Only one carrier there [at a time]. Not in the Taiwan Strait."[7]

The US government also sent official protests to the Chinese government, with Secretary of State Warren Christopher calling the PRC's actions "reckless" and a White House spokesman stating that Washington was "deeply disturbed by this provocative act."[8] The US Congress resolved that in the face of overt threats by the PRC against Taiwan and consistent with the commitment of the US government under the Taiwan Relations Act, the United States would continue

---

3 Patrick E. Tyler, "As China Threatens Taiwan, It Makes Sure U.S. Listens," *The New York Times*, January 24, 1996.
4 Author interview, February 14, 2007, Virginia Beach, VA.
5 Michael Richardson, "Asia Looks to U.S. to Protect Trade Routes around Taiwan," *International Herald Tribune*, March 14, 1996.
6 Author interview, February 14, 2007, Virginia Beach, VA.
7 Author interview, February 14, 2007, Virginia Beach, VA.
8 Patrick E. Tyler, "China Signaling U.S. That It Will Not Invade Taiwan," *The New York Times*, March 13, 1996.

to supply Taiwan with defensive weapons systems. These included naval vessels, aircraft, and air defense, all of which are crucial to the security of Taiwan. The Congressional resolution further stated that the "United States is committed to the military stability of the Taiwan Straits and United States military forces should defend Taiwan in the event of invasion, missile attack, or blockade by the People's Republic of China."[9]

Similar to the Taiwan Strait crises during the 1950s, the US decision in 1995–96 to send aircraft carriers to Taiwan clearly had a profound effect upon Chinese strategic thinking. According to Vice Admiral Lyle Bien, USN (Ret.), commander of Carrier Group 7, who was embarked in USS *Nimitz* during 1996, the Chinese were "very embarrassed by their inability to respond to our presence and so much of their anti-access capability developed since 1996 is precisely in response to this event."[10] Rear Admiral James P. Wisecup, captain of USS *Callaghan* (DDG 994) in 1996, said he could imagine—had the shoe been on the other foot—the type of meeting that might have occurred after such an incident, with China's leaders demanding of the PLAN: "I want to know what you are doing to make sure that never happens again."[11]

Lesson: The US Navy's show of force in the Taiwan Strait helped de-escalate cross-strait tensions. China's strong-arm "missile blockade" tactics backfired, both with regard to the outcome of the Taiwanese presidential election and the US decision to intervene. However, the PRC's failure to counter American aircraft carriers in and around the Taiwan Strait region in 1995–96 has almost certainly contributed to PLAN efforts to buy and build a formidable arsenal of area-denial capabilities. These have included ballistic missiles, conventional submarines, modern combat aircraft, and guided missile destroyers equipped with supersonic anti-ship missiles. Their goal is to ensure

---

9 104th Congress, 2d Session, H.Con.Res. 148, March 7, 1996, https://www.congress.gov/bill/104th-congress/house-concurrent-resolution/148/text (accessed June 23, 2019).
10 E-mail communication with VADM Lyle Bien, USN (Ret.), March 23, 2011.
11 Interview with RADM James P. Wisecup, March 8, 2011.

that in the future outsiders cannot so easily interfere with a Chinese "domestic" dispute. The PRC's acquisition of high-tech sea-denial weapons has undoubtedly increased the risk to US military forces, so the US Navy's "hard power" has arguably been used more selectively since the mid-1990s.

Chapter 14

THE EP-3 STANDOFF AND DIPLOMATIC RESOLUTION (2001)

Diplomacy with China can avoid war. When a US EP-3 surveillance plane was forced to land on Hainan Island after a collision with a Chinese fighter plane, US Ambassador Joseph W. Prueher conducted ten days of intensive negotiations with Beijing to bring about the release of the plane's crewmembers. To end the crisis, Prueher submitted a letter to Beijing, stating, "Please convey to the Chinese people and to the family of pilot Wang Wei that we are very sorry for their loss. [...] We are very sorry the entering of China's airspace."[1] In English, the word sorry does not necessarily imply responsibility. In the Chinese translation of Prueher's letter, however, it did: "The Prueher letter is translated by Chinese officials as both *feichang bao qian*, or 'very sorry,' and *wan xi*." Meanwhile, "a copy of the US Embassy Chinese translation of the same letter only uses *wan xi*."[2] This letter placated China, which led to the release of the American crew. Prueher later explained that much of negotiating with China is building ladders to let them climb down from untenable positions.

Summary of the April 1, 2001 EP-3 Incident

On April 1, 2001, following a collision between a Chinese and American plane, the damaged US EP-3 surveillance plane landed on Hainan Island without permission from the Chinese authorities. The

---

1 http://www.theguardian.com/world/2001/apr/11/china.usa2 (accessed June 23, 2019).
2 http://www.csmonitor.com/2001/0412/p1s2.html/(page)/4d (accessed June 23, 2019).

plane and its crew were immediately detained. To resolve the EP-3 standoff, former US admiral and at that point the US ambassador to China, Joseph Prueher, worked closely with Annapolis classmates, including Richard Armitage, Secretary of State Colin L. Powell's deputy at the State Department, and Admiral Denny Blair, who was CinCPac. At one crucial stage of the negotiations, Admiral Blair offered to send an aircraft carrier to China. This would normally have been Prueher's favored solution, as shown by his actions in 1995–96. But the ambassador declined this suggestion, fearing that too strong a signal might backfire and lead to the prolongation of the incident.[3]

Almost exactly ten days after the April 1, 2001, collision between a US EP-3 surveillance plane and the Chinese jet fighter, Ambassador Prueher delivered the final draft of what became known in Washington as the "Two Very Sorries Letter" to Beijing officials with the message that it would be the Bush administration's best and final offer.[4] In his letter to Chinese Foreign Minister Tang Jiaxuan, Prueher said, "Please convey to the Chinese people and to the family of pilot Wang Wei that we are very sorry for their loss. We are very sorry the entering of China's airspace and the landing did not have verbal clearance."[5] Prueher's letter cleared the way for the return of the EP-3 crewmembers, as well as scheduling a meeting between US and Chinese officials to discuss the incident, consider recommendations for avoiding future such mishaps, and develop "a plan for prompt return of the EP-3 aircraft."[6]

Missing from Prueher's letter was a US apology acknowledging blame for the incident. In fact, "apology" and "responsibility" were words initially demanded by Beijing to settle the incident, but Prueher had made

---

3 David E. Sanger and Steven Lee Myers, "How Bush Had to Calm Hawks in Devising a Response to China," *New York Times*, April 13, 2001.
4 Craig Gordon and William Douglas, "The Crucial Word: 'Sorry'," *Long Island Newsday*, April 12, 2001; Published accounts of this incident include John Keefe, "Anatomy of the EP-3 Incident, April 2001," CNA report (January 2002), and Dennis C. Blair and David B. Bonfili, "The April 2001 EP-3 Incident: The U.S. Point of View," in Michael D. Swaine, Zhang Tuosheng, Danielle F. S. Cohen, eds., *Managing Sino-American Crises: Case Studies and Analysis* (Washington, DC: Carnegie Endowment for International Peace, 2006).
5 "Homeward Bound," *Washington Times*, April 12, 2001.
6 Robert J. Caldwell, "Getting Tougher with Rival China," *San Diego Union-Tribune*, April 15, 2001.

it clear that the US government would "have a problem" with apologizing, since in his judgment as an experienced carrier and test pilot the faster Chinese jet, traveling too close for safety, caused the collision with the slower, propeller-driven EP-3. Ignoring the facts behind the collision, however, the Chinese news media described the US letter as a Chinese victory, with the *People's Daily* reporting, "The firm struggle by the Chinese government and people against U.S. hegemony has forced the U.S. government to change from its initial rude and unreasonable attitude to saying 'very sorry' to the Chinese people."[7]

Notably, there was no official Chinese-language version of Prueher's letter, a deliberate tactic that allowed the Chinese government to spin the facts in their favor. The US embassy provided its own Chinese translation of the letter, however, which rendered the letter's use of "sincere regret" as *chengzhi de yihan*, a close equivalent of the English. Then the letter stated to "please convey to the Chinese people and to the family of Pilot Wang Wei that we are very sorry for their loss." This time, "very sorry" was translated as *feichang wanxi*, an expression of sorrowful condolences, but not one implying culpability.[8] Finally, the letter used *feichang baoqian*, or extremely sorry, for the plane's landing without Chinese clearance.[9]

Since Prueher's letter was written only in English, this gave Chinese officials room to present their own interpretation. Nowhere did a full-fledged "apology"—*daoqian*—appear in the English version of the letter or in the Chinese translation released by the US embassy. However, the Chinese Foreign Ministry translated very sorry as *shenbiao qianyi*, an expression of sincere apology or regret that Chinese linguists say involves an acknowledgment of error and an acceptance of responsibility.[10] The term *qianyi* implied a "deficiency in the U.S. side."[11] According to Mei Renyi, director of the American Studies Center at Beijing Foreign Studies University, "if they're

---

7 "Homeward Bound," *Washington Times*, April 12, 2001.
8 Erik Eckholm, "Chinese Claim a Moral Victory, Describing a Much Bigger Battle," *New York Times*, April 12, 2001.
9 Rowan Scarborough, "Beijing Says U.S. Admits Responsibility in Letter," *Washington Times*, April 12, 2001.
10 Philip P. Pan and John Pomfret, "American Crew Heads Home; China Accepts Letter of Regret," *Washington Post*, April 12, 2001.
11 Scarborough, "Beijing Says U.S. Admits Responsibility in Letter."

translating it that way, especially in the context of a formal letter, it means the U.S. is admitting it was wrong."[12]

Admiral Prueher's two "very sorrys" letter made it possible for the Chinese government to save face while backing off from confrontation. To cover up the differences in translation, Chinese officials and the state-run TV never released the English-language letter. Prueher's creative use of linguistic ambiguity helped solve this Sino-US dispute. It was also better to have the "very sorrys" uttered by Prueher, an outgoing ambassador chosen by former president Clinton, rather than by the current Secretary of State Colin Powell, or by President George W. Bush, which made the letter of lesser political importance.[13] Prueher's letter contained careful phrasing—in English only—that allowed both sides to claim victory.

Lesson: The chance of an accidental collision escalating into a severe Sino-US incident was avoided through the diplomatic use of vague terminology that meant one thing in English and another in Chinese. Prueher judged correctly: "This is not about an airplane, it's about face, and China needs a signal that it is taken seriously."[14] But Beijing's continuing insistence that the April 1 collision was the EP-3's fault and that it occurred in Chinese airspace was not a winning position, especially considering the relative speeds of the two airframes. Therefore, Prueher refused to agree to China's interpretation of events. According to Prueher, negotiating with China, therefore, is really a job of "building ladders for Chinese to climb down."[15] After Beijing's initial outrageous position, Prueher needed to find a graceful way for Beijing leaders to back down, eventually leading to the "two sorrys" letter that the Chinese could interpret as a formal apology, while the U.S. interpreted it as merely a polite expression of regret.

---

12 John Pomfret, "Resolving Crisis Was a Matter of Interpretation," *Washington Post*, April 12, 2001.
13 Jack Kelly, "The Honorable Ending: Bush Avoids the Full Kowtow in China Standoff," *Pittsburgh Post-Gazette*, April 15, 2001.
14 Elisabeth Rosenthal, "China Gets White House's Attention, And Some Respect," *New York Times*, 12 April 2001.
15 Bruce A. Elleman, "The right Skill Set; Joseph Wilson Prueher," in *Nineteen Gun Salute: Case Studies of Operational, Strategic, and Diplomatic Naval Leadership during the 20th and Early 21st Centuries*, edited book, with John B. Hattendorf (Newport: NWC Press, 2010), 230–242.

CONCLUSIONS: THE INFLUENCE OF HISTORY ON THE FORMATION OF A MODERN CHINESE NAVY

Based on the 14 historical case studies discussed earlier, this study has sought to show some of the special characteristics that might impact the behavior of the contemporary Chinese navy. History influences all nations, but some more so than others. Arguably, China is one of the most retrospective nations on the planet, which means Chinese often utilize examples from their past to form contemporary strategies. These historical cases may be applied to new circumstances. A number of the most important historical characteristics will be highlighted in the following sections.

One of the most obvious Chinese characteristics is "face" as in "losing face" and "gaining face." Because of the extreme "loss of face" involved with military defeat, later generations might chose not to dwell on valuable military lessons that might have otherwise been learned. For example, in 938 the Vietnamese used a clever ambush on the Bạch Đằng River to destroy an invading Chinese fleet. Three hundred and fifty years later, in 1288, the Vietnamese used the same ruse a second time with equal success, this time against a Mongol-led Chinese fleet. This second victory was only possible because the Han Chinese admiral never told his Mongol co-commander the history of the 938 defeat, so the Mongol admiral fell into the exact same trap. The highly selective use of historical lessons to favor one's successes over one's defeats occurs in other countries, of course, but seems to be more prevalent in "face" cultures like China.

Another critical Chinese characteristic is the belief in Mandate of Heaven, or the widespread perception that political legitimacy can switch from one dynasty to another succeeding dynasty. Most, but not all, Han Chinese accept the new dynasty without question and will fight for it, regardless of whether the new dynasty is Han or foreign. During the early Yuan dynasty, for example, it was not Mongols fighting in the massive sea battles to dominate China but primarily Han fighting Han. This occurred because of the widespread perception that the Mandate of Heaven had shifted from the Song to the Yuan dynasty. Thus, in one of China's largest sea battles at Yaishan in 1279, it was Han Chinese who carried out most of the fighting on both sides, with the Mongols the ultimate victors. In a similar fashion, most Han Chinese accepted the Communist regime without question in 1949; should this regime ever fall before a rival, however, then the successor government would most likely also be accepted by the majority of Chinese.

An equally important military lesson linked to Mandate of Heaven is that size does not always determine victory in Chinese naval battles. Chinese history has repeatedly shown that the larger fleet with the bigger ships does not always win. In 1363, for example, a smaller but more mobile Ming fleet destroyed a rival on Lake Poyang. Taking advantage of their greater mobility, and by making full use of fireships, the Ming were victorious. To Han Chinese, the counterintuitive outcome of this battle reflected Heaven's approval of the Ming. After all, the Ming victory was critical for the unification of all Han Chinese against their Mongol overlords, leading to the eventual victory of the Ming over the Yuan dynasty. Over five hundred years later, at the Battle of the Yellow Sea, the smaller, but more mobile, Japanese navy defeated its Qing opponent, which to many Han Chinese showed that Heaven did not support the Manchu dynasty; within sixteen years, that dynasty had collapsed in the 1911 Revolution.

Using navies to advance an imperialist agenda based on the tributary system has also been common throughout Chinese history. China is usually described as a land-based, or continental, country. But Chinese dynasties have used naval expeditionary warfare to expand their overseas empire in Southeast Asia for over five hundred years. Contrary to Chinese claims that its intentions have always been friendly, relations with China's southern neighbors have not always been peaceful. In 1410, for example, a Chinese fleet led by Zheng He arrived in local waters near Sri Lanka. When King Alakeshvara of the kingdom of Kotte interfered with his goal of establishing Chinese power and security along the maritime routes, Admiral Zheng He and his troops invaded Kotte, conquered its capital, took its king and his family hostage, and returned with them to China; by the time King Alakeshvara returned home, a more pro-Chinese king was on the throne. In a similar pattern, the PLAN's 1974 invasion of the Paracel Islands, which it took away from the US ally South Vietnam, showed how a naval expeditionary force could be used to extend the Chinese claims.

Offshore islands have often played important military roles. Taiwan, in particular, has repeatedly become a sanctuary for the losing side in Chinese civil wars. Ming loyalists made full use of smaller offshore islands like Jinmen and the Penghus as stepping stones to retreat to Taiwan in the seventeenth century. By fortifying these island bases, they held out against the Manchu invaders for almost forty years. Counting Dutch control of the island during 1624–61, Taiwan was separated from China for 59 years before a naval fleet under Admiral Shi Lang managed to retake it in 1683. The year 60 is extremely important in the traditional Chinese calendar, since it is considered to represent a complete sexagenary (stem-branch) cycle. To have exceeded 60 years might have given the impression that Taiwan's temporary separation was permanent, implying its full independence from China. Now that modern-day Taiwan has been independent for 70 years, perhaps its de facto autonomous status will finally be accepted by the PRC; this might lead to a negotiated settlement, similar to one of their previous United Fronts from the 1920s or 1930s. If this does not happen, however, then any PRC attempt to take control of various strategic offshore islands will almost certainly signal the first stage of an anti-Taiwan invasion.

Ethnic differences have played an especially important role throughout Chinese history, with especially clear divisions not just among Han Chinese, Tibetans, and Uighurs, but also between Han Chinese emperors and foreign rulers. This means that military events in China are often more complicated than they may at first appear, especially given the mix of races and the possible impact of foreign intervention. For example, during the early nineteenth century, the Han Chinese merchants in Canton (modern-day Guangzhou) supported free trade with the British, in opposition to the Manchu Court's desire to control all foreign trade. Because the Manchus, a "barbarian" ethnic group, had established their rule over China by force, many Han Chinese merchants were secretly willing to ally with the British foreigners against their own central government. One of the most complicated battles in the first Opium War (1839–42) was between Han Chinese-manned naval ships working for the Manchus who were assisting a British merchant ship that had signed the Manchu "no opium" ban in opposition to a British fleet, supported by local Han Chinese merchants, which was attempting to stop the Western ship from entering port. In a similar manner, in modern-day China, merchants and businessmen might find that their commercial interests are much closer to foreign partners than they are to Beijing.

Regional differences are a constant problem throughout Chinese history. Almost fifty years after the Opium War, during the Sino-French War (1884–85), the French fleet handily defeated China's Fujian fleet. France had to fight only a fraction of China's total navy, since the northern fleet refused to aid the south. This divide-and-conquer strategy allowed France, which had a small naval presence in Southeast Asia at this time, to defeat China, a much larger opponent. Ten years later, the southern fleets repaid the north by refusing to come to its assistance against Japan. Regional loyalties, a focus on provincial defense rather than national defense, plus political distrust among the different naval fleets, greatly facilitated France's and Japan's victories over China. In the modern period, China's naval forces are still divided into three regional fleets, and it is unclear how well they would cooperate with each other during wartime.

Problems adopting modern technology have been a constant challenge throughout Chinese history. During the late nineteenth century, China first began to buy Western naval technology. But the Chinese attitude toward its foreign-purchased naval equipment was very different from the norm in the West. Rather than using China's military equipment to its full potential to achieve victory, the Qing dynasty adopted severe punishments if equipment was damaged or lost. Mindful that their necks were on the line, during the Sino-Japanese War (1894–95) Chinese officers sought to conserve valuable naval equipment rather than use it. This attitude undoubtedly helped the Japanese win the war, since they used their modern equipment to its full potential. Today, Chinese regulations designed to conserve valuable military equipment might inadvertently mean that sailors are not sufficiently trained to be able to use this equipment in battle. Chinese military leaders can just as often be extremely wasteful, especially if other characteristics—like face—take precedence. Forty years after the Battle of the Yellow Sea, the Chinese attitude toward preserving foreign-made equipment appeared diametrically opposite; much valuable naval equipment was wasted during the second Sino-Japanese War. For example, jealousies between different fleet commanders meant that more Nationalist navy ships were scuttled in the Yangzi River than needed to be. In one particularly infamous case, Admiral Ch'en Shao-kuan, who was planning to sink two of his ships to block the Japanese movement upriver, insisted his counterpart match his two-ship sacrifice so that Ch'en would not "lose face." Four ships were sunk when two might have been sufficient. As a result, valuable foreign-made naval equipment was perhaps needlessly wasted.

Another important Chinese characteristic impacting its naval forces is mutiny. Naval mutinies have played an inordinately important role in Chinese history. For example, in 1949 Stalin told Mao Zedong not to cross the Yangzi River. Many outside commentators assumed that China would be divided into an equal-sized Communist North and a Nationalist South. However, the February 1949 mutiny and defection of the Nationalist flagship *Chongqing*, followed two months later by the mutiny of the bulk of the Yangzi fleet, allowed the Chinese Communists to cross the Yangzi River and take control of all of Mainland China. Once the People's Republic of China was founded on October 1, 1949, this larger-than-expected state soon competed with the USSR over control of the international Communist movement. Because of the constant fear of mutiny, however, Chinese regional fleets are arguably designed to balance each other, and can be pitted against each other if there is a mutiny in order to reassert central control.

Foreign military intervention can also play a crucial role in determining Chinese naval conflicts. While the US Navy elected not to intervene in the Chinese Civil War, during the 1950s the US-backed Nationalist naval blockade plus a US strategic embargo produced dramatic effects on the Chinese mainland. By cutting off the majority of China's foreign trade with the West, the PRC had little choice but to turn to the Soviet government. Two Taiwan Strait crises, the first in 1954–55 and the second in 1958, eventually led to the end of the blockade, in part due to the signing of a secret agreement between John Foster Dulles and Chiang Kai-shek. This agreement was kept secret so that Chiang could "save face." However, economic tensions between the PRC and the USSR had already been exacerbated by the blockade to the point of breaking and this resulted in a Sino-Soviet split during the late 1950s.

Another notable example of foreign intervention occurred in 1995–96 when the US Navy came to Taiwan's aid during a PRC "missile blockade" of the island. In addition to sending one aircraft-carrier battle group through the Taiwan Strait in 1995, which was the first time since 1979 that a major US Navy ship had used this sensitive route, in 1996 a second carrier battle group was recalled from the Persian Gulf. As a result of the US Navy presence, the PRC missile tests were halted earlier than originally planned. Rather than exerting decisive political pressure on Taiwan, the PRC's strong-arm tactics backfired both with regard to the US government and with regard to the outcome of presidential election on Taiwan.

Foreign decisions not to intervene can sometimes produce equally critical long-term changes in the balance of power. A good example of this occurred in 1974, when the US Navy decided not to get involved in the Paracel Island dispute between the PRC and South Vietnam, which was a US ally at the time. This is a good example of "negative space," or something that should have happened but did not happen. As a direct result of this conflict, the PRC took these strategic islands from South Vietnam just a year before Vietnam's unification under the North. It is highly likely that the US government decided to stand aside and not intervene because it wanted to ensure that a newly unified Vietnam did not give its ally, the Soviet navy, access to the port facilities on these strategic islands.

Finally, creative diplomacy can sometimes resolve military logjams. Sino-US relations were tense throughout the rest of the 1990s and spiked following the EP-3 incident on April 1, 2001. After a midair collision, a US EP-3 surveillance plane landed on Hainan Island without first obtaining permission. The plane and crew were then

CONCLUSIONS 79

detained by the PRC. Admiral Joseph Prueher, the US ambassador to China, was in charge of negotiations to free the crew. Rather than resorting to force, he chose to use diplomacy. A more serious military incident was avoided through his clever use of vague terminology to convey an apology that meant one thing in English and another in Chinese. This diplomatic ploy resulted in the release of the American crewmembers.

During the last twenty years the PLAN has grown quickly, but it continues to embody many of the special characteristics of past Chinese navies. Pertinent examples relating to face, Mandate of Heaven, and ethnic and regional differences can be seen over and over again. Whereas the Chinese tend to focus on size, and assume that the largest navy will win, the Battle of Lake Poyang shows that size is not everything. Rather, it is efficient coordination of available naval assets that matters most. Five centuries later, in 1894, a large Chinese fleet was defeated by a much smaller, but more agile, Japanese fleet during the Battle of the Yellow Sea. This single Japanese victory arguably changed the naval balance of power in Asia, since it ceded China's unquestioned hegemony over East Asia to Japan.

While today's PLAN looks large on paper, history suggests that smaller regional navies—such as the Japanese Maritime Self Defense Force or even the Taiwanese navy—could still prove more than a match for the Chinese navy in an actual battle. The best example of inadequate jointness was the 1894 Battle of the Yellow Sea, China's first major naval engagement against another rising sea power. The lack of a unified naval command, in large part to dissuade a naval mutiny attempting to overthrow the central government, is potentially one of the most important historical characteristics. The use of political commissars is another. Specifically, the current division of the PLAN into three regional fleets might present divide-and-conquer opportunities, especially if these fleets cannot react jointly to an attack, or are slow to react because of the dual command structure.

Foreign intervention in Chinese affairs has often been a determining factor. Foreign powers have made use of naval blockade, strategic embargo, and economic sanctions to apply pressure on Beijing, with varying degrees of success. The most notable victory was coordinating the Nationalist blockade and the US strategic embargo during the 1950s to interdict the PRC's foreign trade, thus forcing China to trade almost exclusively with the USSR and Eastern Europe via the Trans-Siberian Railway. This policy had the long-term effect of pushing China and the Soviet Union closer together, thereby increasing mutual economic and political tensions that ultimately resulted in a split.

Other US Navy interventions, such as during China's 1995–96 "missile blockade" of Taiwan, have countered Chinese attempts to put pressure on Taiwan. In all such cases Beijing was forced to back down. But sometimes a decision not to intervene can be even more important, such as when the US Navy stood by during 1974 and did not intervene when China took the Paracel Islands away from South Vietnam. Given the context of the Cold War, and the imminent victory of North Vietnam over South Vietnam, the decision made in Washington was to allow one new ally, China, at this point working closely with US forces against the USSR in the Cold War, to take the islands from an older ally, South Vietnam.

Astute diplomacy can sometimes replace the need for foreign military intervention. During the aftermath of the EP-3 collision on April 1, 2001, and the plane's unauthorized landing on Hainan Island, Ambassador Prueher—born and raised in Tennessee, so no stranger to the importance of honor—on purpose gave China "face" by agreeing to express regret in his "two sorrys" letter. The clever use of vague terminology meant that while the American version of the note did not accept responsibility for the collision, the Chinese-language note issued by Beijing appeared to do so. It was also signed by the outgoing Ambassador Prueher, not by the US president or another high government official.

Since 2001, there has often been an uneasy peace between the US Navy and the PLAN, especially in waters bordering China. Although Beijing argues they are historic waters, the PRC is currently conducting an imperialistic policy in the South China Sea by building island bases. The history of Chinese imperialism in Southeast Asia could be exploited to form anti-Chinese coalitions, as well as to create new multilateral security structures that would work to the benefit of all parties, even China's, once it realizes that trade in the South China Sea is more important than territory. Currently, in the South China Sea island disputes, there is a tug-of-war between those in China who want to adopt a military solution and those who support continued globalization and increased world trade. Given these choices, the US government should actively support Chinese merchants against the militarists.

Meanwhile, contemporary PRC efforts to create a series of island bases in the South China Sea threaten to replicate the kinds of tensions that existed during the 1950s over the offshore islands in the Taiwan Strait. Fearful of a repeat of history, such as when Zheng He's fifteenth-century treasure fleets participated in the Ming–Kotte War, many of China's neighbors to the south might decide to increase cooperation with Japan, India, and the United States to act as possible counterweights to China. Meanwhile, Taiwan and the PRC are probably considering closer cooperation to obtain their common territorial objectives in the South China Sea. A more thorough understanding of how Chinese historical characteristics and peculiarities impact modern-day policy makers in Beijing, and especially those special characteristics that distinguish the Chinese navy, could assist these countries in picking suitable maritime counterstrategies to deal with an apparent renewal of Chinese maritime expansion.

SELECTED BIBLIOGRAPHY

Accinelli, Robert, *Crisis and Commitment: United States Policy toward Taiwan, 1950–1955* (Chapel Hill: University of North Carolina Press, 1996).
Ballantine, Joseph W., *Formosa: A Problem for United States Foreign Policy* (Washington, DC: Brookings Institution, 1952).
Barlow, Jeffrey G., *From HOT WAR to COLD: The U.S. Navy and National Security Affairs, 1945–1955* (Stanford, CA: Stanford University Press, 2009).
Bate, H. Maclear, *Report from Formosa* (New York: E. P. Dutton, 1952).
Blechman, Barry M., and Berman, Robert P., *Guide to Far Eastern Navies* (Annapolis, MD: Naval Institute Press, 1978).
Bush, Richard C., *At Cross Purposes: U.S.-Taiwan Relations since 1942* (Armonk, NY: M. E. Sharpe, 2004).
Chang, Gordan H., *Friends and Enemies: The United States, China, and the Soviet Union, 1948–1972* (Stanford, CA: Stanford University Press, 1990).
Chang, Pao-Min, *Sino-Vietnamese Territorial Dispute* (New York: Praeger, 1986).
Chen Jian, *Mao's China & the Cold War* (Chapel Hill: University of North Carolina Press, 2001).
Chen Ming-tong, *The China Threat Crosses the Strait: Challenges and Strategies for Taiwan's National Security*, trans. Kiel Downey (Taipei: Dong Fan Color Printing Co., 2007).
Chiu, Hungdah, *China and the Taiwan Issue* (New York: Praeger, 1979).
Christensen, Thomas J., *Useful Adversaries: Grand Strategy, Domestic Mobilization, and Sino-American Conflict, 1947–1958* (Princeton, NJ: Princeton University Press, 1996).
Clough, Ralph N., *Island China* (Cambridge: Harvard University Press, 1978).
Cohen, Warren I., ed., *New Frontiers in American-East Asian Relations* (New York: Columbia University Press, 1983).
Dikötter, Frank, *Mao's Great Famine: The History of China's Most Devastating Catastrophe, 1958–1962* (New York: Walker, 2010).
Dulles, Foster Rhea, *American Policy toward Communist China, 1949–1969* (New York: Thomas Y. Crowell, 1972).
Eastman, Lloyd E., *Throne and Mandarins: China's Search for a Policy during the Sino-French Controversy* (Cambridge, MA: Harvard University Press, 1967).
Eisenhower, Dwight D., *The White House Years: Mandate for Change, 1953–1956* (Garden City, NY: Doubleday, 1963).

———, *The White House Years: Waging Peace, 1956–1961* (Garden City, NY: Doubleday, 1965).

Elleman, Bruce A., *Modern Chinese Warfare, 1795–1989* (London: Routledge, 2001).

Elleman, Bruce A., and Christopher Bell, eds., *Naval Mutinies of the Twentieth Century: An International Perspective* (London: Frank Cass, 2003).

Elleman, Bruce A., and S. C. M. Paine, eds., *Naval Blockades and Seapower: Strategies and Counter-Strategies, 1805–2005* (London: Routledge, 2006).

Elleman, Bruce A,. and John B. Hattendorf, *Nineteen Gun Salute: Case Studies of Operational, Strategic, and Diplomatic Naval Leadership during the 20th and Early 21st Centuries* (Newport: NWC Press, 2010).

Elleman, Bruce A., and S. C. M. Paine, eds., *Naval Power and Expeditionary Warfare: Peripheral Campaigns and New Theatres of Naval Warfare* (London: Routledge, 2011).

Elleman, Bruce A., and James Bussert, *People's Liberation Army Navy (PLAN) Combat Systems Technology, 1949–2010* (Annapolis, MD: Naval Institute Press, 2011).

Elleman, Bruce A., and S.C.M. Paine, *Modern China: Continuity and Change 1644 to the Present*, Second Edition (Lanham, MD: Rowman & Littlefield, 2019).

Elleman, Bruce A., *Taiwan's Offshore Islands: Pathway or Barrier?* (Newport, RI: NWC Press, 2019)

Falkenberg, Rainer, *Constantin von Hanneken: Briefe aus China 1879–1886* (Koln, Germany: Bohlau Verlag, 1998).

Gallagher, Rick M., *The Taiwan Strait Crisis* (Newport, RI: Strategic Research Department, Research Report, 1997).

Garthoff, Raymond L., ed., *Sino-Soviet Military Relations* (New York: Frederick A Praeger, 1966).

Garver, John W., *China's Decision for Rapprochement with the United States, 1968–1971* (Boulder, CO: Westview Press, 1982).

———, *The Sino-American Alliance: Nationalist China and American Cold War Strategy in Asia* (Armonk, NY: M. E. Sharpe, 1997).

Gibert, Stephen P., and William M. Carpenter, *America and Island China: A Documentary History* (Lantham, MD: University Press of America, 1989).

Goodspeed, M. Hill, *U.S. Navy: A Complete History* (Washington, DC: Naval Historical Foundation, 2003).

Gu, Weigun, *Conflicts of Divided Nations: The Case of China and Korea* (Westport, CT: Praeger, 1995).

Hickey, Dennis Van Vranken, *United States-Taiwan Security Ties: From Cold War to beyond Containment* (Westport, CT: Praeger, 1994).

Hinton, Harold C., *China's Turbulent Quest* (New York: Macmillan, 1972).

Holober, Frank, *Raiders of the China Coast: CIA Covert Operations during the Korean War* (Annapolis, MD: Naval Institute Press, 1999).

Holt, Edgar, *The Opium Wars in China* (Chester Springs, PA: Dufour Editions, 1964).

Hood, Steven J., *Dragons Entangled: Indochina and the China-Vietnam War* (Armonk, NY: M. E. Sharpe, 1992).

Inglis, Brian, *The Opium War* (London: Hodder and Stoughton, 1976).

Kerr, George H., *Formosa Betrayed* (Boston, MA: Houghton Mifflin, 1965).

Khrushchev, Nikita Sergeevich, and Sergei Khrushchev, *Memoirs of Nikita Khrushchev: Statesman, 1953–1964* (University Park, PA: Penn State Press, 2007).
Kierman, Frank A., Jr., and John K. Fairbank, eds., *Chinese Ways of Warfare* (Harvard, MA: Harvard University Press, 1974).
Kissinger, Henry, *White House Years* (Boston, MA: Little, Brown, 1979).
Kondapalli, Srikanth, *China's Naval Power* (New Delhi: Knowledge World, 2001).
Lasater, Martin L., ed., *Beijing's Blockade Threat to Taiwan: A Heritage Roundtable* (Washington, DC: Heritage Foundation, 1986).
Levathes, Louise, *When China Ruled the Seas: The Treasure Fleet of the Dragon Throne, 1405–1433* (New York: Oxford University Press, 1994).
Li, Xiaobing, *A History of the Modern Chinese Army* (Lexington: University of Kentucky, 2007).
Lilly, James R., and Chuck Downs, eds., *Crisis in the Taiwan Strait* (Washington, DC: American Enterprise Institute for Public Policy Research, 1997).
Liu, Ta Jen, *U.S.-China Relations, 1784–1992* (Lanham, MD: University Press of America, 1997).
Lo, Jung-pang, *China as a Sea Power, 1127–1368* (Singapore: NUS Press, 2012),
Lüthi, Lorenz M., *The Sino-Soviet Split: Cold War in the Communist World* (Princeton, NJ: Princeton University Press, 2008).
Marolda, Edward J., "The U.S. Navy and the Chinese Civil War, 1945–1952," Ph.D. Dissertation, George Washington University, 1990.
———, *A New Equation: Chinese Intervention into the Korean War. Proceedings of the Colloquium on Contemporary History* (Washington, DC: Naval Historical Center, 1991).
———, *The Approaching Storm: Conflict in Asia, 1945–1965* (Washington, DC: Government Printing Office, 2009).
McGiffin, Lee, *Yankee of the Yalu: Philo Norton McGiffin, American Captain in the Chinese Navy (1885–1895)* (New York: E. P. Dutton, 1968).
Morris, Stephen J., *Why Vietnam Invaded Cambodia: Political Culture and the Causes of War* (Stanford, CA: Stanford University Press, 1999).
Muller, David, *China as a Maritime Power* (Boulder, CO: Westview Press, 1983).
Nguyen, Van Canh, *Vietnam under Communism, 1975–1982* (Stanford, CA: Hoover Institution Press, 1983).
Park, Chang-Kwoun, "Consequences of U.S. Naval Shows of Force, 1946–1989," Ph.D. Dissertation, University of Missouri-Columbia, 1995.
Powell, Ralph L., *The Rise of Chinese Military Power, 1895–1912* (Princeton, NJ: Princeton University Press, 1955).
Rawlinson, John L., *China's Struggle for Naval Development, 1839–1895* (Cambridge, MA: Harvard University Press, 1967).
Ray, Hemen, *China's Vietnam War* (New Delhi: Radiant, 1983).
Reardon, Lawrence C., *The Reluctant Dragon: Crisis Cycles in Chinese Foreign Economic Policy* (Seattle: University of Washington Press, 2002).
Ross, Robert S., ed., *After the Cold War: Domestic Factors and U.S.-China Relations* (Armonk, NY: M. E. Sharpe, 1998).

Ryan, Mark A., David M. Finkelstein, and Michael A. McDevitt, *Chinese Warfighting: The PLA Experience since 1949* (Armonk NY: M. E. Sharpe, 2003).
Schell, Orville, *Mandate of Heaven* (New York: Simon & Schuster, 1994).
Schreadley, Richard L., *From the Rivers to the Sea: The United States Navy in Vietnam* (Annapolis, MD: Naval Institute Press, 1992).
Shen, James C. H., *The U.S. & Free China: How the U.S. Sold Out Its Ally* (Washington, DC: Acropolis Books, 1983).
Shu Guang Zhang, *Economic Cold War: America's Embargo against China and the Sino-Soviet Alliance, 1949–1963* (Stanford, CA: Stanford University Press, 2001).
Swaine, Michael D., Zhang Tuosheng, Cohen, Danielle F. S., eds., *Managing Sino-American Crises: Case Studies and Analysis* (Washington, DC: Carnegie Endowment for International Peace, 2006).
Swanson, Bruce, *Eighth Voyage of the Dragon: A History of China's Quest for Seapower* (Annapolis, MD: Naval Institute Press, 1982).
Synder, Edwin K., A. James Gregor, and Maria Hsia Chang, *The Taiwan Relations Act and the Defense of the Republic of China* (Berkeley: University of California Press, 1980).
Szonyi, Michael, *Cold War Island: Quemoy on the Front Line* (New York: Cambridge University Press, 2008).
Tkacik, John J., Jr., ed., *Reshaping the Taiwan Strait* (Washington, DC: Heritage Foundation, 2007).
Tsai, Shih-Shan Henry, *Maritime Taiwan: Historical Encounters with the East and the West* (Armonk, NY: M. E. Sharpe, 2009).
Tucker, Nancy Bernkopf, ed., *Dangerous Strait: The U.S.-Taiwan-China Crisis* (New York: Columbia University Press, 2005),
Tyler, William Ferdinand, *Pulling Strings in China* (New York: Richard R. Smith, 1930).
Wang, Gabe T., *China and the Taiwan Issue: Impending War at Taiwan Strait* (Lanham, MD: University Press of America, 2006).
Whiting, Allen, *China Crosses the Yalu: The Decision to Enter the Korean War* (New York: Macmillan, 1960).
Wittfogel, Karl, *History of Chinese Society: Liao (907–1125)* (Philadelphia, PA, 1949).
Womack, Brantly, *China and Vietnam: The Politics of Asymmetry* (New York: Cambridge University Press, 2006).
Yang Zhiben (杨志本), ed., *China Navy Encyclopedia* (中国海军百科全书), vol. 2 (Beijing: Sea Tide Press (海潮出版社), 1998).
Young, Marilyn, *The Vietnam Wars, 1945–1990* (New York: HarperCollins, 1991).
Yu, Peter Kien-hong, *The Four Archipelagoes in the South China Sea* (Taipei: Council for Advanced Policy Studies, 1991).
Zhao Suisheng, ed., *Across the Taiwan Strait: Mainland China, Taiwan, and the 1995–1996 Crisis* (New York: Routledge, 1999).

INDEX

Aegis cruiser 65
Africa 21
Aju 12
Alakeshvara 21–22, 75
Annam. *See* Vietnam
Annapolis 1, 70
Arabs 8
Armitage, Richard 70
Art of War 7
Asia Minor 11
Ataqai 13
Aurora 47, 48
Austria 11

Bạch Đằng River 7–10, 73
Baillie-Grohman, Captain 44
barbarian 3, 4, 26, 34, 76
barbarian management 3, 4, 34
Battle of Bạch Đằng River 7–10
Battle of Chuanbi 29–34
Battle of Kowloon 32
Battle of Lake Poyang 17–19, 79
Battle of the Yalu 39
Battle of the Yellow Sea 39–42, 74, 77, 79
Battle of Yaishan 11–16, 74
Bayan 13
Beijing 12, 21, 29, 30, 32, 33, 34, 37, 56, 58, 59, 60, 64, 69, 70, 71, 72, 76, 79, 80, 81
Beijing Foreign Studies University 71
Beiyang fleet 35, 36, 39–42
Bien, Lyle 66

Blair, Denny 70
blockade 1, 17, 31, 32, 45, 51–56, 63–67, 77–81
blockships 43–46, 51, 77
Bo Hai 52
Bohai Gulf 48
Bolsheviks 4
Britain 29–34, 39, 44, 47, 48, 53, 54, 76
Brunei 19
Burma 3
Bush, George W. 70, 72

Cairo declaration 63
Cambodia 55
Canton. *See* Guangzhou
Central Kingdom. *See Zhongguo*
Ch'en Shao-kuan 44–46, 77
Chen Youliang 17–19
Chen Yuan 41
Chiang Kai-shek 27, 34, 44, 46, 47–50, 51–56, 78
China Year Book 46
Chinese Communist Party 5, 30, 47–50, 52, 77
Chinese Foreign Ministry 58, 70, 71
Chinese Imperial Navy 42
Chongqing 49
Chongqing 47–50, 77
Christopher, Warren 65
Clinton, Bill 72
Cochin 21
Cold War 80

continental country 4, 11, 23, 74
Cornell University 63
Courbet, Admiral 35–37

Dachen Islands 51, 53, 56
Dai Viet. *See* Vietnam
Daidu 12
Dalian 48
Daoguang emperor 29, 30, 32
Daya Islands 13
Deng Xiaoping 59–60
diarchy 1, 4
Ding Ruchang 19, 40
Ding Yuan 40–41
Dinghai Island 33
diplomacy 4, 5, 30, 69–72, 78, 79, 80
Dong Wenbing 12–13
Dulles, John Foster 54–55, 78
Dutch 25–27, 75

East Asia 11, 13, 79
East China Sea 19
Eastern Europe 80
Eisenhower, Dwight D. 54
Elliot, Charles 31–32
Elman, Benjamin A. 36
embargo 1, 51, 56, 77–78, 79
EP-3 collision 37, 69–72, 78, 80
ethnic 1, 3, 8, 10, 23, 75, 76, 79
exclusion zone 64
expeditionary warfare 21, 22, 23, 26, 27, 32, 57–61, 74, 75

face, gaining and losing 1, 4, 5, 7, 9, 10, 45, 49, 50, 51, 72, 73, 77, 78, 79, 80
fireship 18
foreign trade 30, 31, 56, 76, 78, 80
Formosa 25
Formosa Resolution 54
France 35–37, 41, 76
Freeman, Chas 64–65
Fujian fleet 76
Fujian province 27

Fuzhou 13, 35–37, 52
Fuzhou Harbor 35
Fuzhou shipyards 35, 36

Grand Canal 33
Great Leap Forward 51
grog 1
Guangdong Navy 30, 44
Guangdong province 8, 59
Guangzhou 8, 13, 29, 30, 31, 32, 33, 36, 76
Guangzhou fleet 8, 36

Ha Long Bay 9
Hai Chen 45
Hai Chi 45
Hai Chou 45
Hai Rong 45
Hainan Island 13, 37, 52, 57n1, 70, 78, 80
Hainan province 61
Hainan Straits 8
Han state 17–19
Hang Dau Go 9
Hangzhou 12, 13
Hong Kong 31–33
Hongwu emperor 18
Huludao 48
Hungary 11
Hyacinth 29

Imjin River 11
Independence 65
India 21, 30, 33, 53, 81
Indian Ocean 21, 22, 64
Indonesia 19
intervention 1, 5, 34, 53, 57, 60, 61, 63, 65, 66, 75, 77–80

Japan 1, 2, 19, 25–26, 27, 36n1, 39–42, 43–46, 64, 76–77, 79, 81
Japanese Imperial Navy 19, 39–42, 43–46, 74, 79

INDEX

Japanese Maritime Self Defense
   Force 79
Japanese pilots 1
Java 21
Jiangyin forts 45
Jinmen Island 26, 27, 51–56, 65, 75
Johnson Reef 61
jointness 19, 29, 37, 42, 50, 54, 79
Jones, John Paul 1
junks 29, 32–33, 43, 52, 54

Kangwha 11
Korea 3, 11, 47, 51
Korean War 51, 52, 53
Kotte 21–24, 75, 81
Koxinga. *See* Zheng Chenggong

language 1, 71–72, 80
Lee Teng-hui 63
Leizhou Peninsula 13
Li Heng 14–15
Li Hongzhang 35–39
Lin Zexu 30–34
Lin Zun 49
Liu Buchan 40
Liu Hongcao 8–9
Liu Shen 13
Liu Yan 8
Liu Zheng 12, 16
Liuqiu. *See* Okinawa
lou chuan 18
Louisa 32
Luerman 26

Macclesfield Bank 61
Mainland China 2, 16, 47, 50, 53, 77
Malacca 21–22, 23
Malaysia 19, 22
Manchuria 2, 3, 48
Mandate of Heaven 1–5, 11, 16, 47,
   49, 50, 74, 79
Mao Zedong 4, 5, 49, 51, 55, 58, 77
Mawei Harbor 36
Mazu Islands 53, 54, 56, 65

McGiffin, Philo Norton 40n3
Mei Renyi 71
Mikura 43
Ming dynasty 17–19, 21–24, 25–27,
   74, 75, 81
Ming-Kotte War 21–24, 81
Mishima 43
missile blockade 63–67, 78, 80
Mongol yoke 4
Mongolia 3, 58
Moravia 11
Muslim 3
mutiny 5, 47–50, 77, 79

Nan-Han 7–10
Nanjing 22, 26
Nanyang fleet 35, 37
Nationalist Navy 2, 43–46, 47–50,
   51–53, 77, 79
Nationalists 45, 47–50, 51–55
negative space 61, 78
Nehru, Jawaharlal 53
Netherlands. *See* Dutch
New York Times 64
Ngô Quyền 7–10
Nimitz 64, 65, 66
Ninghai 43, 45
Nixon, Richard 57, 58
North Vietnam 57–61, 80
nuclear war 64

Okinawa 3
Opium 29–34, 76
Opium War 29–34, 76
Outer Mongolia 58

Paek River 7
Palmerston, Lord 31–32
Paracel Islands 57–61, 75, 78, 80
parachute 1
Paris 1
Patenôtre, Jules 37
Pearl 32
Pearl Harbor 36n1

Pearl River 13, 31
Pengchiayu Island 63
Penghu Islands 26, 27, 54, 75
People's Daily 71
People's Liberation Army (PLA) 1, 49, 52, 53, 58, 59
People's Liberation Army Navy (PLAN) 2, 4, 5, 26, 42, 49, 50, 54, 57–61, 66, 75, 79–81
People's Republic of China (PRC) 2, 24, 26, 27, 29, 37, 47–50, 51–56, 57–61, 63–67, 75, 77–81
Perry, J. C. 41
Persian Gulf 21, 65, 78
Pescadores. *See* Penghu Islands
Philippines 19
Pinghai 43, 45
pirates 13, 21, 22, 25, 26, 27
Poland 11
political commissar 1, 4–5, 79
Polo, Marco 4
Port Arthur 36n1, 41
Portuguese 25
Potsdam Conference 63–64
Powell, Colin L. 70, 72
Poyang Lake 17–19, 74, 79
Prince Guang 13
Prince Yi 13
Prueher, Joseph 65, 69–72, 79, 80

Qianlong emperor 3
Qifu 48
Qing dynasty 2, 3, 4, 25–27, 29–37, 39–42, 50, 74, 76
Quanzhou 13
Qubilai Khan 4, 12
Quemoy. *See* Jinmen Island

Rawlinson, John 36
RC-135 Rivet Joint 65
Rebellions 2, 3, 8
Red Army 58
regionalism 35, 41
Republic of China (ROC) 51, 53
Robertson, Walter S. 55
Royal Navy 1, 29
Royal Saxon 32
Russia 3, 4, 11, 48
Ryukyu. *See* Okinawa

sanctions 1, 79
scurvy 33
secret diplomacy 5, 54, 56, 78
Seventh Fleet 52
sexagenary cycle 27, 75
Shandong province 42, 48
Shantou 52, 54
Shi Lang 27, 75
short-range ballistic missile (SRBM) 64
Siam 21
Sihanouk, Norodom 55
Silesia 11
sinify 3
Sino-French War 35–37, 41, 76
Sino-Japanese War I 39–42, 76
Sino-Japanese War II 43–46, 77
Sino-Soviet border 60
Sino-Soviet friendship treaty 60
Sino-Soviet split 56, 58, 78
Sino-Vietnamese War 58–61
Song dynasty 9, 11–16, 30, 74
South China Sea 19, 21, 22, 24, 27, 58, 60, 61, 80–81
South Vietnam 57–61, 75, 78, 80
Southeast Asia 21–24, 56, 74, 76, 80
Soviet Union. *See* USSR
Spratly Islands 22, 60, 61
Sri Lanka 21–24, 75
Stalin, Joseph 47, 49, 60, 77
Sullivan, Walter 48
Sunzi 7

Tainan 26
Taipei 54, 64
Taiwan 2, 3, 16, 19, 25–27, 47, 50, 51–56, 57n1, 63–67, 75, 78, 79, 80, 81

INDEX

Taiwan Relations Act 65–66
Taiwan Strait 2, 5, 16, 25–27, 51–56,
    63–67, 78, 81
Tang dynasty 7–8
Tang Jiaxuan 70
Tatan Island 52
Thailand 3
Tianxia 2–3
Tibet 3, 8
Tongking 8
torpedo boats 36, 44
tower ship 18
Tran Hung Dao 9
Trans-Siberian Railway 80
treasure fleet 21, 22, 23, 81
tributary system 1, 3, 4, 7, 8, 21,
    23, 35, 74
Truman, Harry 52
Turks 8
two sorrys letter 72, 80
Tyler, William 40

US Asiatic Fleet 48
US Navy 1, 51–52, 54, 57, 61,
    63–67, 77–80
Uighurs 3, 8, 75
United Daily News 64
United Front 2, 75
United States 2, 34, 46, 53, 54, 58,
    61, 65–66, 81
USSR 2, 5, 16, 34, 47, 51, 56, 57–58,
    60–61, 77, 78, 80

Vietnam 3, 7–10, 15, 19, 23, 35–37,
    57–61, 73, 75, 78, 80
Volage 29, 32

Wang Shiqiang 13
Wang Wei 69–72

Weihaiwei 42
Wenzhou 52, 54
White Falcon 13
White House 65
Wisecup, James P. 66
wokou 25
World War II 27, 34, 56, 64
Wuhan 12

Xiamen 51, 52
Xinjiang 60

Yaishan 11–16, 30, 74
Yangzi River 12, 17, 26, 29,
    33, 43, 45–46, 47–50,
    52, 77
Yanjing 12
Yatsen 45
Yellow Goose 13
Yingrui 45
Yongle emperor 21, 22
Yuan dynasty 3, 11–16,
    17, 74

Zaiton. *See* Quanzhou
Zeelandia 25, 26
Zhang Hongfan 13–16, 30
Zhang Rongshi 12
Zhang Shijie 13–16
Zhapu 13
Zhejiang province 13, 51
Zheng Chenggong 25–27, 30
Zheng He 21–24, 75, 81
Zhili province 35
Zhongguo 2
Zhou Enlai 55
Zhoushan Islands 52
Zhu De 49
Zhu Yuanzhang 17–19

www.ingramcontent.com/pod-product-compliance
Ingram Content Group UK Ltd.
Pitfield, Milton Keynes, MK11 3LW, UK
UKHW041936210426
5322IPUK00015B/207